jenniemae & james

ALSO BY BROOKE NEWMAN

*The Little Tern*

# Jenniemae & James

### A MEMOIR IN BLACK & WHITE

## Brooke Newman

HARMONY BOOKS / NEW YORK

Published in the United States by Harmony Books, an imprint of the
Crown Publishing Group, a division of Random House, Inc., New York.

www.crownpublishing.com

Harmony Books is a registered trademark and the Harmony Books colophon is a
trademark of Random House, Inc.

Library of Congress Cataloging-in-Publication Data
Newman, Brooke.
Jenniemae & James / Brooke Newman.—1st ed.
p. cm.
1. Harrington, Jenniemae. 2. Newman, James Roy, 1907-1966. 3. Newman,
Brooke—Family. 4. Washington (D.C.)—Race relations—History—20th
century. 5. Men, White—Washington (D.C.)—Biography. 6. African American
women—Washington (D.C.)—Biography. 7. Mathematicians—Washington
(D.C.)—Biography. 8. Women domestics—Washington (D.C.)—Biography.
9. Friendship—United States—Case studies. 10. United States—Race
relations—Case studies. I. Title. II. Title: Jenniemae and James.

F205.A1N49 2010
975.3'0410922—dc22                    2009029721

ISBN 978-0-307-46299-2

Printed in the United States of America

*Design by Leonard W. Henderson*

10 9 8 7 6 5 4 3 2 1

First Edition

*For*

*Nikos, Samantha, Blue, Joey,*

*and for Mark*

*These numbers gonna sing*

*These numbers gonna cry*

*These numbers gonna dance*

*These numbers tell no lie*

—JENNIEMAE HARRINGTON, SONG, 1948

To count is to talk the language of numbers. To count to a googol, or to count to ten is part of the same process; the googol is simply harder to pronounce. The essential thing to realize is that the googol and ten are kin, like the giant stars and the electron. Arithmetic— this counting language—makes the whole world kin, both in space and in time. Mathematics may well be a science of austere logical propositions in precise canonical form, but in its countless applications it serves as a tool and a language, the language of description, of number and size.

—JAMES R. NEWMAN,
*Mathematics and the Imagination*, 1940;
WHEREIN THE TERM "GOOGOL," AKA
"GOOGLE" WAS FIRST DESCRIBED

This book is a family memoir; it is a true story based on my best recollections of the events and times, and the recollections of my family who shared those events and times with me. In some instances, I rearranged and/or compressed events and time periods in service of the narrative, and due to the limitations of my perspective as a child, I was compelled at times to create what I believed was plausible and likely dialogue to bring the actual scenes to life and to match the best available recollections of those events and exchanges.

*jenniemae & james*

# CHAPTER ONE

*"Get up with the sun,*

*get to work by the gun,*

*go to bed when you're done."*

Jenniemae Harrington was an underestimated, underappreci-
ated, extremely overweight woman who was very religious, dirt
poor, and illiterate. She was uneducated, self taught, clever, and
quietly cunning. Born on an unknown day of an unknown
month during the harvest season of 1923 on a small sharecrop-
per farm near Hissop, Alabama, Jenniemae picked October 18 as
her birth date because on that date, at the age of four years, she
had for the very first time been permitted to wear flowers in her
hair to church. It was as memorable a day as any, and a very
good day in a long line of difficult days. There were not many
simple pleasures for the Harrington family, but at least on Sun-
days everyone tried hard to greet the Lord's Day with a smile,
and wearing flowers in one's hair was a special way to celebrate
church day.

Home was the farm. The farm, like most sharecroppers'
farms, was located on the least arable land in the worst loca-
tion—it was land unlikely to produce more than a barely

sustainable crop even if all the atmospheric conditions were perfect. The Harringtons lived in a one-room shanty with enough holes in the roof to collect rain even if there was only a thin mist during the night. Jenniemae was born to Molly and Jefferson Harrington in 1923, one of twelve children. Hissop is a small town not far from Equality, Alabama, which Jenniemae said was exactly what the people who lived there meant to call it when they named it that, because equality down there was a thing for white folks and not at all meant for black folks. As Jenniemae said, "That e-quality ain't nothin' more than a white word, jus' a word—nothin' more, nothin' less, and surely not meant nor 'tended for a colored man." And she was right. The laws there were meant to protect white folk, and all the rest just came to the table when and how they were told.

Hissop was home because it was where Jenniemae's family ended up, not because it was a chosen home site. And Jenniemae told me that if it hadn't been for her father's ill-willed nature, they never would have left.

"Now, if'n it hadn' been for my daddy bein' to who he was, I wouldn' be standin' here right now and takin' care of you childr'n. If we had had us a nice and kind daddy . . . well, then, we would best be livin' down there in Hissop still, to this very day. So what I am sayin' is that a person can't always tell when a bad thing is the cause of a good thing to come, or if a bad thing is jus' always goin' to be a bad thing forever and on."

"What do you mean?" I asked.

"I mean that it was all the cause of the evilness inside my daddy's veins that his blood turned dark and then the blood darkness made him one bad-angry man. Some said his blood went bad from one too many humiliations, which will do it to a man. One too many humiliations can turn a good man into an evil devil. Which is why one night when he was out with his liquor, my mama packed us up and we ran away."

Jenniemae's mother fled their drunk and abusive father and Hissop, Alabama, when Jenniemae was six years old. Of the twelve children born to Molly and Jefferson, Jenniemae was the sixth, which is why the number 6 became her most important, "standin' tall and walkin' out" number. Six played a major role in Jenniemae's life and therefore played a role in our family's lives, because whatever affected Jenniemae affected us. For instance, Jenniemae wore six hair pins to tie back her hair in a bun; she always set rows of six cookies on the cookie plate, rows of six carrots on the carrot plate, and rows of six celery slices on the celery plate; she set up six clotheslines outside to dry the washed wet clothes, and when it was possible, she hung six pieces of clothing on each line. She sang six verses of each song, dusted each bookshelf six times, every book spine six times, and secretly tapped the banister six times as she ascended and descended the staircase.

When Jenniemae's mother left Alabama, she headed north and just kept going. She had nothing more than what she needed—her children and the clothing each one had on his or her back. They planned to live with a cousin who had settled in Washington, D.C. When one of us would ask about those years in Alabama, Jenniemae had little to say. She would tell bits and pieces about the long, hard, hot, and humid days she had spent in the fields picking from the time she could stand up until the time they headed north. "Pickin' cotton, pickin' berries, pickin' beets, pickin' bo-weevils, ants, spiders, chiggers, skeeters, and any other crawlin' and itchin' ugly insect you ever laid your eyes upon. Nope, nothin' to talk 'bout in those times. Nothin' but bent-over, achin' backs and hotness.

"We went up north 'cause. Just 'cause. If a person was to go away to some other place than where they lived, well, then, that person was goin' to go north," she told me. Jenniemae said that her people went to Washington, D.C., because they figured if the president lived there, life for a colored person would be better. In Washington, D.C., they all hoped they could get decent jobs. "Little did they know," she said, "and most over, little didn't they know."

Once they got to D.C. by the back of anything that moved— "Back o' the train, back o' the truck, back o' the back"—the extended Harrington family lived in a run-down, two-room bad excuse for a house located in Foggy Bottom, which today is home to the John F. Kennedy Center for Performing Arts, the State Department, the Department of Interior, and the George Washington University campus. In those days it was an area mostly occupied by the working poor. Since 1860 Foggy Bottom had been a neighborhood where Negroes, as we called African-Americans back then, settled after they fled from slavery and where German and Irish immigrants settled upon arriving in this country. By 1920 the area was the home to the largest Negro business and residential community in the United States. It also became known as the home to Negro jazz and blues entertainers, and Negro intellectuals and artists. It was where Jenniemae grew up and spent most of her childhood.

Fancy automobiles driven almost entirely by white men and women ran along the paved D.C. streets while horse-drawn buggies, driven almost entirely by Negro men, pulled both cargo and people through the bumpy, stone-cobbled roads of Foggy Bottom. When the United States went to war in 1941, everyday life changed for most white people in the country as a result of gas rationing, soaring rents, and rising food prices. But for the black people of Foggy Bottom, life didn't change much at all. As Jenniemae said, "Get up with the sun, get to work by the gun, go to bed when you're done."

# CHAPTER TWO

*"Every family's got more*

*than 'nough problems . . . but only*

*the mule family says they got none."*

Ours was a family that was more or less conflicted, rarely relaxed or easygoing, emotionally wrought, unusual, often unsettling, offbeat, and frequently difficult. My mother, Ruth, had night terrors, migraines, black periods, claustrophobia, and borderline schizophrenia to maneuver. My father, James, had imagined illnesses that were difficult to differentiate from his real illnesses, an insatiable need for a lover other than his wife, a mercurial egotism, a perfectionism, and an almost unmanageable tension created by an intellectual brilliance that frequently threw him into an isolated world. As for my brother, Jeffrey, and me—well, we navigated the complex terrain as best we could. Jeffrey's relationship with our father was extremely tense and often argumentative. They loved each other but had a difficult time finding just how to connect without strife, which was only made more complicated and poignant because of our mother's belief that she needed to protect Jeffrey from the conflicts he had with our father. Jeffrey was neither a quiet nor a loud child.

Two years older than me, he was always—at least in my eyes— the ultimate authority on most subjects. Not only was he extremely quick and bright, he was an exceptional athlete. From an early age he could throw and catch a baseball with remarkable skill and accuracy. He was fast on his feet and quick with his hands. Not unsurprisingly, Jeffrey inherited our father's mathematical gifts, though given their competitive relationship, this would never be a field he would go into. Rather, he used those mathematical skills amassing baseball statistics, which he employed in a complex game he invented. These games filled hundreds of sheets from yellow legal pads that Jeffrey kept in his bedroom, stacked in boxes. The boxes and those yellow pads were so sacred that I never would have dared look through them if not given permission. Just as some people might find solace by playing a musical instrument, I believe my brother found solace in all forms of baseball, whether made-up or real games.

The relationship my brother and I developed was heavily influenced by the particular relationship each of us had with our parents. Depending on the circumstances in the house on any given day, and on the ebbs and flows of our parents' moods, Jeffrey and my connection was either loving, competitive, strained, close, distant, supportive, or frustrating. Like most siblings, we did our best to get along, though there were certainly times when we did not do well together at all. I believe we learned from a very young age to be very cautious of each other's feelings, which unfortunately caused us to frequently live disconnected and separate lives.

I was the quiet child—in fact, I frequently attempted to be the

From right to left Brooke, Jeffrey, and a friend sitting on the stoop in front of our house
*Author's collection*

invisible child—rarely calling attention to myself or creating dissension if I could avoid it. Sidestepping conflict and competition, I grew up choosing to watch rather than participate, and paid a price for that, since as the quiet child, I was also the easy child, often taken for granted. It didn't take long before I learned to create both real and imaginary hideaways, which I assumed would adequately protect me from the disquieting noises, the questionable visitors, the out-of-tune conversations, and the frenzy that defined the conflicts in my environment. By the time

I was seven years old, I had already perfected the art of skipping school by building a camouflaged hideout amid the thick brush in the woods that were just blocks from our house. Instead of going to school each day, I hid amid the brush and trees, watching birds build nests, and squirrels and chipmunks scurry into their own hideouts, and saving countless numbers of worms from drowning on days when it rained. I re-invented my world as I spent day after day there and was forced to give it up only when the school principal finally telephoned to see what had happened to me. I never admitted exactly where I was or what I was doing, and when asked, I lied. No one ever questioned my lie. My mother never asked where I'd been, and since my father had little regard for school—he believed in education but not school in particular—he never pressed the subject. My skipping school really had very little to do with school itself. It wasn't that I hated school, because I didn't, it was simply that I needed an imaginary world more than I needed school. My memories of school are vague but my memories of this and other hideouts are vivid. The upside of these hideaways was that I believed I was protected from the bright glare and noise of the craziness that was going on with my family and I could dissociate from it; the downside was that I believed that I would always be able to dissociate from that world. In fact I saw too much, understood too little, had no skills to interpret what I witnessed and little inclination to articulate it. I do not recall being an unhappy child—I wasn't unhappy—though I do recall often being a lonely child no matter how many friends I had. Mine was a preoccupied family—preoccupied with life, death, outside ene-

Brooke in Truro, Massachusetts
*Author's collection*

mies, and inside demons. Jenniemae—a part of the family soon
after beginning to work in our house—seemed to quickly and
instinctively understand the situation. Perhaps her understanding came from a common empathy bred out of her own past.
Like me, Jenniemae was an observer—she watched, she rumi-
nated, and more often than not she soothed the wounds caused
by our family's tensions, since when it came to problems with
our family, she could choose to step aside from our difficulties
without stepping too far inside our lives.

Jenniemae and James were, without a doubt, two unlikely
companions who developed a unique relationship and remained
loyal and steadfast to each other throughout their lifetimes.
Work brought them together: One was an employer and the

other an employee. They were quickly drawn to each other because each had a quick wit and a good heart, and moreover they had a shared fascination with and attraction to the world of numbers. Jenniemae would have said it was "the Lord's numbers" that gave them a conversation, while James would have said it was the world of mathematics that was their common bond. What began with a mutual enjoyment with numbers soon turned into a mutual respect, a quiet love and true admiration for each other.

Jenniemae did pretty much everything in the house that needed to be done. She dusted, swept, mopped, and vacuumed the four-story house we lived in, she washed the clothing we wore, hung out the wet clothes on long backyard lines, ironed, fluffed the pillows, made the beds, shopped for the food, served and cooked all the meals (which included a formal four-course dinner each night), baked the cookies, pies, and cakes, sewed buttons, patched pants, reset hems, took care of my older brother and me from the time I was four and he was six on through our college years, dusted the more than forty thousand books my father amassed, fed the dogs, cats, and birds, and was more frequently than not the adviser and moral compass of our home. In other words, Jenniemae was a nanny, maid, nurse, and adviser, all in one person. On top of all that, she was a perfectionist. What had to be done had to be done absolutely 100 percent right. If it wasn't perfect, it had to be done again and again until it was. That perfectionism carried over from her personal appearance into her work. She was, above and beyond everything else, tidy.

Two aspects of her life, however, were not completely con-
trolled and tidy. One had to do with her habit of playing the
numbers. Jenniemae played the illegal lottery almost every
single day of her life. The lottery Jenniemae played was called
policy, which was code for the illegal lottery that first began in
Chicago in 1885 by a man called Policy Sam. Policy bets were
derived from number groups that ranged between 1 and 78. A
two-number combination was called a "saddle," a three-number
(the most common bet) was a "gig," and a four-number combination was called a "horse." The numbers were frequently picked,
as was true for Jenniemae's picks, by their connection to dreams.
Dream numbers (which derived from African-American hoodoo
tradition) linked images to meanings, which in turn were linked
to numbers. For instance, if Jenniemae had a dream about butter,
then she knew it meant there might be sadness along with good
luck coming her way, and a butter dream was attached to the
numbers 4, 7, and 13. If she had a dream about the policy office
where the bets were placed, then this implied that good fortune
might soon come her way. The numbers attached to dreaming
about the policy office were 4, 11, and 44.

The list of dreams and their meanings and the appropriate
numbers connected to those dreams were written in books and
pamphlets that were bought and passed from person to person.
Since Jenniemae couldn't read, she had set to memory these
important facts. And she added one more twist to the dream
numbers and policy bets: She created her own list of numbers
that she attached to dream images and meanings—not because
she saw herself as particularly prescient but rather because she

simply had "the feeling" that a certain dream brought on a certain meaning, and that meaning was attached to a number. Moreover, that number wasn't something she just pulled out of thin air—she believed that the numbers were directly and purposely sent to her by the Lord Himself. Jenniemae explained that the Lord had decided to bestow on her this one small gift since she was a loyal believer who lived a sparse life amidst a world of plenty. She used to say, "God loveth and giveth to those who sing His praises by bein' a loyal believer." Many other people agreed with her on this matter—they, too, thought she had been given the gift of numbers by the Lord since there was no other explanation why it came to pass that more often than not Jenniemae won the policy bets.

Besides policy, Jenniemae liked to play bingo at her church and cards with friends. When she wasn't playing the Lord's numbers or card games, Jenniemae was a penny-pincher who took great pride—and enjoyment—in seeing how much could be saved on anything bought. Some of that penny-pinching was out of necessity, but much of it was out of a love for watching numbers shrink and grow. She pinched pennies for her own well-being and for that of our family, even when it wasn't necessary.

The other aspect of her life that escaped her control was her weight. Jenniemae was woefully overweight by about two hundred pounds or more, depending on the month, and her weight exacerbated her arthritis. She had frequent and painful attacks of arthritis and asthma, though she would rarely talk about these ailments. She was usually an optimist but also a realist.

She was almost always good humored, quick witted, could be a harsh though extremely patient critic, enjoyed lavishing praise on others (particularly children), was shy, loving, and was never loved enough. She had one boyfriend, named John-John, on and off throughout her life. John-John weighed less than half of what Jenniemae weighed, drank too much, ate too little, and was never there when she needed him. Her family, friends, nieces, nephews, our family, policy, her work, her Baptist church in southeast D.C., and the church choir: These were the most important things in her life. Illiterate, uneducated, and extraordinarily clever, Jenniemae had a remarkable ability to make the best out of a bad day or a bad year or a bad life. Some people pray to make things better, some people eat or sing or dance to the tune, and Jenniemae did do all of those things, but the one thing that seemed to work best for her on a daily basis was policy betting on her dream number, and doing that made a bad day feel a whole lot better.

Although James's life wasn't remotely similar to Jenniemae's, he understood trying to make the best of bad days. For a number of reasons his was never an easy life. Born in 1907 in New York City to two Jewish immigrants—his mother, Eugenie, was from Czechoslovakia, and his father, Frederick, was from Germany—he had an older sister by seven years, Madeleine, with whom he was never close. James was the only son, an unexpected gift to the family during very difficult years when money was short. After arriving in America, his father, a surgeon by training, worked in a deli on the Upper East Side of Manhattan until he received an American medical license.

He ultimately became a surgeon at Lenox Hill Hospital, where he played a prominent role in establishing the city's first tuberculosis treatment center. Tuberculosis was a fairly common disease in the early twentieth century. So, too, were scarlet fever and rheumatic fever. And even though James's father's specialty was respiratory diseases, he almost lost his only son to both of them.

It was 1911, just before James's fourth birthday, when he came down with scarlet fever, which within weeks led to acute rheumatic fever. For days James experienced prolonged high fevers, severe joint pain, nosebleeds, and chest pains. No matter that his father was a physician, there was no cure other than good care mixed with love and a bit of luck. His mother cared for him around the clock, but nevertheless the inflammation wreaked havoc on his system and caused severe and permanent damage to his heart valves. The doctors the family consulted did not expect James to live through the ordeal, and his parents were advised that if he lived a month, it would be a miracle. He did survive that first month, however, and even made it through a year. But he remained sick during the second year with an extremely compromised immune system, carditis (heart inflammation), and periodic high fevers. Month after month the doctors continued to predict that he would not live long, given the damage already done to his heart. But the second year passed and then another, and James did survive, probably in part because of his doting mother, who sat by his bedside, changing damp sheets, soothing his aches and pains, reading to him and playing the piano, which she did very skillfully. For over two years

James was bedridden, living day by day. Instead of succumbing to the disease, though, eventually he became healthier. But despite his recovery, James would live under a cloud of impending heart failure and premature death throughout his life. As a child he was always cautioned about being around other people; he was limited in his athletic activities and spent much of his youth indoors, where his mother supplied him with books and music and his father taught him the game of chess. Nevertheless, every day brought the real possibility that he would not live to see the next day.

In addition to his ill health, James had the very questionable fortune of being pegged as a genius. He was said to have been a mathematical prodigy at the age of five, could multiply double-digit numbers in his head, had an understanding of square roots, and by the age of seven was placed on street-corner soap boxes in New York City and asked to perform mathematically. Crowds were said to have gathered on the corner of Forty-second Street and Broadway to listen to him recite mathematical puzzles and tricks. IQ tests suggested that he had an IQ of 175. When he began school he was skipped from grade to grade until he entered City College in New York at the age of fourteen. He completed the usual four-year college curriculum in a similarly abbreviated fashion and entered Columbia Law School. Too young to practice law after passing the New York State Bar Exam, he then went to graduate school at Columbia for mathematics and philosophy.

Because James was always far younger than his classmates, he became somewhat of a social outcast. That, combined with the pessimistic longevity forecast that always haunted him, unquestionably influenced his relationships with women. James threw himself into these relationships as if there might be no tomorrow, or certainly no day after tomorrow. He jumped into love with the same intensity with which he'd approached his education. In 1925, at the age of eighteen, he married a shy young woman who was a student at City College. Since neither had money or a job, they lived with his parents in their two-bedroom apartment on East Eighty-sixth Street. They divorced six months later when she discovered he was having an affair, and not too very long after that—when he was twenty—he married for the second time. That marriage also ended in divorce within a couple of years. By the time he was twenty-four, he had married a third time. Outside affairs ended that relationship, too.

At age thirty he got married for the fourth time, this time to the woman who would be my mother, Ruth May Gallert. Ruth was a very bright, energetic twenty-three-year-old New Yorker who was living alone and working as a remedial-reading teacher at various Manhattan schools. Having gone to Rutgers University (then called the New Jersey College for Women) and having won numerous awards for her poetry, she had visions of a career in writing, but, the combination of her lack of finances, her entering the work force during the Great Depression, and the dubious possibility that a female writer could earn a living precluded her from following that dream. Most women who needed to work during this period were limited to careers in education or to secretarial work, and Ruth chose education.

It didn't hurt that she was also a very attractive woman—something that came in handy in finding a job and, as well, in meeting men. She was in almost all ways a quite petite woman, with small hands, small feet, a tiny waist, small hips, and delicate facial features—in fact, the only large part of her body was her bust. She had honey-colored blond hair usually worn in a stylish bob and unusual green eyes, a deep sea-green color with tiny specks of brown. People—both men and women—were quick to notice her remarkably beautiful complexion, a smooth, silky ivory coloring that brought unwanted attention, given how uncomfortably shy she was. Ruth had very conflicted emotions about being sexually attractive, on the one hand, but unsure and insecure, on the other. She forced herself to be social but preferred to be alone, having little confidence in her own ability to make and then maintain close friendships. She confided to me once that her very best friends in life were her cigarettes—she smoked four packs a day (a habit she began at the age of fourteen)—and those cigarettes loyally kept her company every day and every night.

Unfortunately, Ruth—no matter how bright, clever, artistic, adventurous, and attractive—was never enough for James. He had to have other women in his life besides his wife—possibly because he needed more praise than one woman could give, possibly because he would never trust any one woman and two offered more security, possibly because his appetite was never satiated, possibly because he was egotistical, or possibly because he had a sadness and a fear and a disquiet that could not easily be resolved. In any case, he had more lovers than anyone would

Ruth in Truro, Massachusetts
*Author's collection*

have wished to count. I personally knew of twelve or fourteen—
particularly the five who lived with us under the same roof
over the years, which my mother seemed not only to agree with
but also to encourage, as she and the live-in lovers stayed up late
many nights playing card games or Scrabble or discussing her
husband/their lover, as if they might one day together—lover
and wife—figure out what made the man they both knew and

loved tick. Why Ruth not only put up with but also encouraged these lovers was a bewilderment, though in its own twisted fashion it was understandable. Given how timid and apprehensive, vulnerable and uncertain she was, it was easy to fathom why she might encourage problematic relationships, particularly relationships wherein boundaries between people were blurred. Boundaries that might have existed were chipped away and often nonexistent. Patients sometimes became friends, colleagues could become lovers, lovers might become live-ins, her own children often became both consultants and advisers, and her husband sometimes took on the role of a live-in neighbor. Boundaries—the distinction between what should and should not occur between people—implied rejection for Ruth, and rejection was something she wanted no part of. She neither wanted to be rejected nor wanted to reject others. She allowed people to cross over into her life in ways they should not have, and she, too, crossed over into other people's lives in ways that were inappropriate. Life for Ruth was often a balancing act between the person she thought she should be and the person she really felt she was. Perhaps most people have at least two sides to their personalities, but for Ruth these two sides frequently seemed diametrically opposed, were constantly battling for attention, were impossible to deny and frequently impossible to hide. No matter how calm or collected she might appear on the outside, Ruth was an extremely tense, worried, frustrated, and incomplete woman who spent much of her life trying to find answers that would ultimately make her feel complete. After years of working as a remedial-reading teacher, she chose a career in

Ruth at Balston Beach, Truro, Massachusetts
*Author's collection*

mental health in large part because of her wish to find these answers. And her deep empathy for the emotional turmoil other people felt would allow her to become an extremely capable and successful clinical psychologist, though ironically she never quite figured out how to apply her reasoning and depth of understanding to her own life and that of her family's.

James was likely drawn to Ruth because of all these qualities. He liked bright, quick, witty, crazy, beautiful women who were also vulnerable and seemed somewhat needy. His approach to life was edgy and voracious, and not only did he go through both school and women quickly, he also amassed a fairly thick professional résumé by the time he was in his late thirties. For a short while he practiced law, but disliking its tedium, he soon left the profession. From 1938 to 1944 he served as Chief Intelligence Officer at the U.S. Embassy in London. From 1944 to 1945 he was the Assistant to Undersecretary of War Robert Patterson, and from 1948 until 1952 he was the Special Counsel to the Congressional Committee on Atomic Energy, where he had a leading role in drafting legislation to establish civilian control over atomic energy. Following the war he served as the Deputy Director of the Office of War Mobilization and Reconversion. In 1946 he was awarded a Guggenheim Fellowship for his work on the history of science. And for many years he worked closely with Albert Einstein on the atomic energy issue until Einstein's death in 1955.

In 1940 his and Edward Kasner's book, *Mathematics and the Imagination*, was published. It was in this book that the definition of the mathematical concept of a very large but finite number which they called "googol," and another larger number called "googolplex" was first presented for mass publication. One day almost sixty years after googol's conception, and close to forty years after my father's death, two Stanford students borrowed the word, changed the spelling to "google," and used it as a Web site, a financial conglomeration, a verb, a noun, and an adjective. Indeed, my brother and I grew up learning that the term "googol"—which was by no means a commonly used word until the 1990s—did not emanate from the imagination of Edward Kasner's nephew, as was described in *Mathematics and the Imagination*. Rather it was a silly word fashioned by a number of children in a kindergarten class in Manhattan that my father was visiting. They suggested it when he asked them for a word to describe a very large number that was just shy of infinity, or just shy of forever and ever. However, when writing the book, our father thought that attributing the word to Kasner's nephew would make a quaint connection.

In 1942, James's book *The Tools of War* was published, a thorough, illustrated examination on the mechanics of warfare that offered a glimpse into history by looking at weaponry. In 1948 he published *The Control of Atomic Energy*; in 1955, *What Is Science?* appeared; and in 1956 he completed the four-volume bestseller *The World of Mathematics. Godel's Proof* came out in 1958, *Science and Sensibility* in 1961, *The Rule of Folly* in 1962, and *The Harper Encyclopedia of Science* in 1963. During these years he was also an editor at *Scientific American* magazine and a competitive chess player who on a number of occasions was known to have played games with five people simultaneously while blindfolded. Though many have described him as a mathematician, he never felt quite comfortable with that description. He liked to invent mathematical games and also to play established number games; he enjoyed doing numerical calculations and toying with statistical probabilities; he obsessively struggled with unsolved formulas for weeks and months or years and enjoyed watching already so-called solved formulas unravel—but he did not see himself as a mathematician. He loved to write numbers down on pieces of paper—simple, straightforward numbers—and see how those simple numbers could work magic when combined with other numbers, but he did this for fun as if they were children's blocks to be toyed with or chess pieces to be moved about.

My father kept many secrets. Some concerned his work and

some his personal life. He rarely discussed what he did on any given day and almost never spoke about his past. My father died when I was twenty-one, and I can't recall his ever mentioning his own father, Frederick, who died in 1940 in San Francisco while visiting his daughter, Madeleine. His father lay in a coma for three weeks and James, who was stationed in London at the time, was unable to see his father before he died. James never mentioned a word about this or what his father had been like as a man or as a physician or as a deli worker.

I remember his speaking about his mother, Eugenie, a person with whom he was very close, only once, and that occurred long after she had died. We were sitting around the dinner table one evening when my father said in passing, "Today would have been my mother's birthday." He said nothing further, and neither my mother nor my brother or I would have dared ask him to, knowing he wanted to end the conversation there. Sharing past family history was not something he ever cared to do. There was never talk about when or from where his parents had immigrated or where they had grown up or who their relatives were or what they were like, though we knew the original family name had been changed from von Neumann to Newman. Other than this it was as if his entire past had been erased. Perhaps because they were immigrant Jews or perhaps because of something else, it all remained unspoken territory. Nor did my father ever discuss his older sister, Madeleine Reichert, who lived with her rabbi husband in San Francisco and was not involved in any part of my life. Both past family and Judaism were taken for granted but never mentioned. We were—because he was—Jewish atheists, though our mother was secretly religious. Not until years after he died would she admit that she believed in God, and it was only then that she began to attend services at a local D.C. synagogue. James would never have denied he was a Jew, but he had an absolute disdain for all religious rites, groups, and beliefs. His antireligious attitudes had more to do with his belief in science, evolution, and the practical than it did with social necessity or the need to hide who or what he was.

James was a meticulous man who dressed formally and stylishly. His suits were all tailor-made in London, his silk ties were all bought from a specialty store in New York. His shirts were French and required cuff links, which were either made of gold or embedded with diamonds. He shined his Italian leather-crafted shoes every time they were worn. He kept his closets perfectly neat, and his dresser drawers were lined and immaculately kept with socks and underwear, which Jenniemae knew to set in perfect rows and ordered by color. My father demanded perfection. He kept his office the same way, books placed on the shelves by their subject matter, yellow pads neatly stacked on the desk corner, pens neatly kept in ink wells, and trash cans emptied regularly. His mind may have been overloaded and spinning with ideas, but his desk would always be neat.

He had a sense of humor and was not afraid of mistakes—sometimes he relished them, in fact, seeing in them an opportunity to solve another problem. He was irreverent, outspoken, and exceptionally literate both about subjects that interested him and those that did not. He read books voraciously, about mathematics, physics, chess, birds, turtles, the wind, the moon, the stars, foreign countries, elephants, anteaters, desert spiders and cacti, civil rights, dictatorships, birthing, diseases, automobiles, trains, and even grape nuts. He loved well-made machines, particularly automobiles, and then particularly race cars. When affluent, he owned Aston Martins (a DB5, a DB6, and a DB7), Facel Vegas, and Ferraris. He had his cars detailed weekly, and no one got into them without first thoroughly cleaning their shoes. He loved well-made watches and owned a large collection of them—Swiss, German, Austrian, and English. He enjoyed dining out at fine restaurants, especially with his girlfriends. He loved to drink, especially I. W. Harper bourbon, and tended to overdo it on many occasions. He smoked Chesterfield cigarettes and could smoke a pack a day or not smoke for a week or two. He had hobbies—he loved to play tennis, which he did fairly well though he didn't care too much about winning or losing, he enjoyed horseback riding though he rarely did it, he was passionate about chess, enjoyed collecting stamps and buying rare books. He loved animals, particularly big dogs, and we always had one or two English setters or golden retrievers, who were usually named after literary figures (there was Molière, Flaubert, and Chekhov) or musicians (Mozart, Bach, and Beethoven). The man was complex and compassionate, with too much and too little of an ego.

His friendships were few but extremely loyal. He was competitive, difficult, and sometimes impossible with friends and colleagues. When wronged, he never forgot, and when he disliked someone, he relished making their lives miserable.

James
*Photo by Philippe Halsman*
*© Halsman Archive*

His mind never stopped spinning, formulating, and refiguring—he could never give it a rest. While considering a subject—whether a new formula he was working on or the current political landscape—he would pace back and forth, frequently talking to himself, mumbling what seemed to be half sentences, completely disengaged from the rest of the world.

Given how very different Jenniemae and James were, their story, which began as a simple employment contract, turned into a most unlikely relationship. It is said that opposites attract and sometimes it is said that similarities attract, but with these two people neither saying applied. They were not exactly opposites and they clearly did not have many similarities—save for their obsession with the world of numbers and their loyalty, love, and respect for each other.

# CHAPTER THREE

*"Only a fool will argue against the sun."*

Jenniemae came to work for our family in the autumn of 1948. The night before, my parents fought bitterly. It had nothing to do with her—at least not directly. It had to do with Virginia, the woman she was replacing.

"Virginia's a drunk," my father barked.

"She drinks but she's not a drunk," my mother argued.

"What would you know?"

"About drinking or about Virginia?"

"About either. Virginia is a damned drunk and you choose to ignore that minor fact because it makes your life easier," my father said. "It suits you to be blind to what is going on in this house no matter the cost to your children."

"You think my life is easy. You wouldn't have any idea of what I do every day. You pay no attention because that suits you."

"We're not talking about your life now, we're talking about the goddamned drunk maid who almost burned the house down— and, by the way, almost set fire to your daughter in the process."

"And that's my fault?"

"Damn, you're impossible. It's not about you. It's about firing the drunk maid."

"You don't have to yell. I know what it's about."

"It is your job to take care of the maid—making sure that the maid isn't going to murder the children would be on that short list."

"Short list? Short list?"

"How hard is it to hire or fire a maid?"

"Go ahead, then. If it's so easy, then you do it."

"That is your job, not mine. Your job." My father had a habit of repeating himself frequently, which my brother said was because he was a "sometimes lawyer" and "sometimes lawyers" repeated themselves more than full-time lawyers. That made sense to me at the time because I was the younger sister and had nothing else with which to compare my brother's analysis.

"My job?" my mother repeated.

"Since you have obviously given up on being a mother, the least you could do is find a sober housekeeper. How hard can that be? How goddamned hard can that small task be?"

"Well, maybe you could ask one of your girlfriends to clean or take care of our children, or are they drunks, too?"

"I'll ask them. Which one would you prefer, the blonde or the redhead?" he said, walking away.

"Son of a bitch!" my mother cried. "You're a son of a bitch."

Arguments like this were not infrequent. Some led to vicious personal attacks and others remained relatively mild mannered. Usually the arguments had a shelf life of no more than

Jeffrey and Brooke
*Author's collection*

twenty-four hours, after which my parents would make up with
as much zest as they had put into arguing. Their seesaw relationship was as hot as it was cold, and there were very few calm
or quiet in-between moods to soften the extremes. They either
loved each other passionately or hated each other viciously.
Even the constant stream of lovers didn't diminish the hot and
cold passions. Maybe they contributed to them, though I have

31

my doubts, because the lovers were always there; like the dogs that slept on the living-room rug, they were just there. My parents didn't fight like couples who have come to know each other well and understand the boundaries of the boxing ring—they fought like two people who were willing to take the bout into the streets. When either one threatened to leave the marriage, it was to be taken seriously. On any given day separation or divorce was a real possibility, even though it wasn't a common practice in the 1940s. The day-to-day "getting along" that I saw in the relationships of my friends' parents never seemed to be a part of my own family's ritual. There were no sweet greetings at the front door at the end of a long day, there was no holding hands walking down the street, or silly private jokes or knowing smiles. For my parents, life was serious business, and love was a serious part of that. The slightest event could and would set them off—buying new shoes, burning the breakfast toast, the paper boy leaving a torn newspaper, a burned-out lightbulb, the dog disappearing, or the maid getting drunk once too often.

Virginia had been the maid and nanny in our house for four years, and had it not been for the fact that she spent more time drinking than working, once tried to choke my brother to death for stealing cookies from the cookie jar, and one afternoon while on a binge almost burned the house (and me) to the ground, she would not have been fired. It is fair to say that Virginia probably could have kept the job if she hadn't passed out on the basement floor while the steaming-hot iron was burning a hole in my father's white shirt. When the shirt and the ironing board burst into flames, I happened to be toddling around under the board.

The only thing that saved me was the mailman, who happened to stop by to "pay Virginia a visit" (an unrelated though common occurrence that Virginia insisted required my naptime and her disappearance into another room). Fortunately, the mailman was sober. He immediately called the fire department, and not too long thereafter three fire engines arrived to put out the fire.

Virginia was fired that afternoon and Jenniemae was hired soon thereafter.

# CHAPTER FOUR

*"Better to eat one cake in peace than two in trouble."*

The year Jenniemae arrived was a pivotal year, both inside our house and around the country. My parents had been married eleven years and had two children. Their arguments about sex, lovers, money, work, and children were overshadowed—at least for my father—by his increasing involvement with issues surrounding the possible proliferation of nuclear weapons. Most Americans were not worrying about the potential uses and abuses of atomic energy—they were celebrating having successfully weathered many difficult years, which included the Great Depression, the Dust Bowl, Pearl Harbor, the death of Franklin D. Roosevelt, and the end of World War II. There was an excitement in the air for many in the country.

By 1948, American families found all sorts of wonderful new electric appliances and gadgets available in stores—irons, coffeemakers, eggbeaters, multi-speed mixers, toasters, furnaces, electric blankets, hair dryers, phonographs, and clocks. In 1948 my family used to gather around our Philco radio and wait for

James holding Brooke and Jeff
*Author's collection*

the quick tempo of Rossini's "William Tell Overture" to intro-
duce the newest broadcast of *The Lone Ranger*. Moments later
we would be greeted with the shrill cheer of, "A fiery horse with
the speed of light, a cloud of dust, and a hearty 'Hi-yo, Silver,
away! The Lone Ranger!'" And so began Brace Beemer, the
voice of the masked Texas Ranger, known as the Lone Ranger,
and his Native American companion, Tonto, played by John
Todd, as the two heroes carried us through another thrilling ad-
venture. Sounds of their horses, Silver (the Lone Ranger's white
horse) and Scout (Tonto's pinto), could be heard snorting and
galloping through Western canyons overtaking the bad guys.
The nights of listening to *The Lone Ranger* were, without a

doubt, some of my fondest memories—the family was together and seemingly peaceful.

For Jenniemae, however, 1948 wasn't likely to seem any different from 1947 or 1937. While men of different creeds and colors had fought side by side just a few years ago, the country was still very divided by race, culture, and class. People who were white and wealthy could enjoy all these new material goods and gadgets, but those who were black or poor were not about to see much change in day-to-day living. The new life was not intended or marketed for the "other" people, though those who worked for the rich would soon have to learn how to use the products. In 1948 civil rights meant white men's rights. And when in that same year President Truman took the leap of faith to suggest that Congress should outlaw lynching, many people thought that the president had lost his mind.

When Jenniemae first started working at our house, my father probably barely noticed her comings and goings. He was far too involved in what he felt were the looming and lethal threats inherent in letting the atomic cat out of the bag, and in just who—the military, the president, an international tribunal, a national committee, or Congress—would control this power. He worked alongside physicists like Albert Einstein, since both of them were passionately involved in the endeavor to promote the peaceful use of atomic energy and warn the public of its inherent dangers. Einstein was then the chairman of the Emergency Committee of Atomic Scientists (ECAS). James became the liaison between the scientists and the policymakers. One of his political allies in this struggle was Helen Gahagan Douglas, a congresswoman from

California. She wrote in her autobiography: "Jim Newman was obsessed by concern that whoever had the bomb would also acquire world dominance, which he believed presented grave risks for keeping the peace. Like me, he hoped to see an international tribunal administer the development of atomic power for the benefit of all nations.... The possibility that the military would control atomic power created an uproar in the scientific community. Physicists turned up everywhere urging that control remain in civilian hands.... Jim Newman was tireless in arranging for scientists to meet with influential congressmen to tell them what atomic power could do. My office became the center of operations."*

But keeping the secrets about how to make an atom bomb, and also not letting the general population know how lethal the bomb was, were difficult, if not impossible, tasks. By 1948 it was evident that the Soviet Union had already gained the necessary information on atomic-bomb building through undercover espionage rings. The possibility that World War III, or "the war to end all wars," might occur sent chills through the circle of people privy to what was going on. It would not be long before the rest of the country would also know. Internal federal investigations soon began to find the spies and traitors who divulged these national secrets. Congress created the House Committee on Un-American Activities, and in the fall of 1948 names of possible traitors began to appear on the lists composed by the committee members. One by one,

---

*Helen Gahgan Douglas, *A Full Life* (New York: Doubleday, 1982), p. 216.

physicists and mathematicians, chemists and biologists, senators, congressmen and -women, actors, directors, artists, and bankers were being investigated for possible connections with Communists or sympathizers with Communism, since these secrets had been divulged to Communist Russia.

Newspapers began running headlines divulging those names. They were all considered to be potential threats to the country. At the top of the "potential spy list" were those individuals who had been involved in the science and the politics surrounding the development of the atomic bomb. Congresswoman Douglas came under scrutiny. The newspapers knew who Douglas was—they even were aware of rumors that she was having an affair with the tall, lanky senator from Texas, Lyndon Johnson. They also picked up on a rumor that Douglas was romantically involved with the meticulously dressed James Newman, who was involved with dialogue concerning the policies and politics of the bomb.

Beginning in 1948 and for the next five years, FBI agents often sat on the stoop across from our house and watched my father's comings and goings. He, in turn, taunted them by playing cat-and-mouse games, making telephone calls on tapped phone lines in foreign languages, and sneaking out of the back of the house to go nowhere in particular. But Jenniemae had already become protective of our family and saw these games in a different light. She chided him for not seeing that The Man could be dangerous.

One morning she reprimanded him: "You out heapin' coals of fire right before their eyes and you don't think they have the eyes to see what's burnin'."

After considering this, he replied, "They may have the eyes to see the fire, but they don't have the minds to figure out what's burning."

"You don't know that, and moreover, it don't take knowin' what's in the fire to be able to put it out. Some put out a fire with water and some put out a fire with more fire. Soon will come the day that those men over there are goin' to try and put out your fire with their own fire."

"Maybe. Maybe you're right."

"That's so, Mister James. That's so. I know I'm right."

# CHAPTER FIVE

*"It's bad luck to leave a chair rockin'*

*when you get up, so be sure to settle it down."*

It didn't take long before Jenniemae and James found a mutual and edgy sense of humor as their paths crossed each day. They both worked in the house—she cleaning and being a nanny and he working on atomic energy policy issues and writing books about science and mathematics. It also did not take long before the family realized that the arrival of Jenniemae Harrington was one of the luckiest things that ever happened to us.

Jenniemae appeared at the back door of the house every morning before the sun rose and left every evening long after the sun went down. She worked six days a week, and even though she weighed well over three hundred pounds and had to walk a mile and a half to and from the bus stop in order to get to our house, she cleaned, washed, ironed, cooked, walked up and down those four flights of stairs numerous times each day, and she rarely complained.

Every morning Jenniemae did two things without fail. First, she would share her saying for the day, which she said was the only way to properly start out the morning. Her sayings came to her, she told us, "as soon as my eyelids flutter and my mind thinks on the day." Most of her sayings were personal re-creations of Bible sermons she had heard and traditional proverbs that had been passed down. All the sayings of the day had one thing in common: They had a purpose. They were not meant as simple suggestions of how to live a better life, they were meant as words of advice or warnings about particularly ominous possibilities that could occur anywhere and anytime to anyone. Some sayings were more serious than others, and those might be delivered five or six times, while other sayings were less important and required only a one-time pronouncement.

The second thing Jenniemae did each morning was to call in her policy number to "the man." Usually her bets were three-digit "gigs," and she would put a penny on each "gig," but sometimes she bet a four-digit "horse," and more often than not she bet on five or six "gigs" or "horses" on any given day. If she won, the payout might be as much as ten to one, and if she won five times during that day, then she surely went about her busi-ness a very happy woman. The winning numbers were picked by the man, or someone working in the policy office, who was the spinner of a large wheel. Frequently the wheel spinner had a name like the Red Devil or Dead Row or Streamliner—names Jenniemae would mention every once in a while when speaking with her sister, Cora, or her boyfriend, John-John, on the phone about that day's wins or losses. Fraud in the policy world was fairly common, because the spinner of the wheel could easily slow or quicken the spin, but that didn't bother Jenniemae or the other thousands of people who played the policy lottery every day around the country.

The wheel was spun more than one time every day, so winning once or twice on any given day was not that unusual, particularly if you placed many bets daily. Winning frequently, however, eight out of ten tries or more, was highly unlikely—and that is exactly what Jenniemae did. She won a high percentage of bets—higher than normal, *much* higher than normal—and although the man didn't suspect anything out of the ordinary, especially given Jenniemae's position as a poor Negro maid from southeast D.C., he also wasn't particularly happy about it, either. On the other hand, Jenniemae's winnings brought her friends and relatives into the betting scheme, and in his mind that probably offset her winnings. So the man left Jenniemae alone and paid out what was due when she won.

As soon as my father discovered that Jenniemae not only played the numbers but also often won, that became the primary item for discussion every morning. Any concerns she might have had that Mister James would be upset with her placing bets on his telephone were soon squelched when she realized he could not have been more thrilled. The very idea that she was playing with and betting on numbers was an absolutely wonderful distraction for him each day.

"You're a gambler," he said to her one morning.

"No, I most certainly am not."

"Sure you are. It's terrific news. Terrific!"

"Is that so?"

"Absolutely."

"Well, I don't gamble, Mister James. That's not what it is."

"You place bets on numbers. Is that right?"

"Well . . . not really."

"Sure you do."

"Well . . . maybe in just a small way."

"Either you do or you don't, and I prefer to think that you do," he said with a smile.

"It's not gamblin', though. It's the Lord's gift."

"Is that right?"

"It is right. The numbers aren't my own. They are the Lord's."

"Which means the Lord must love to gamble!"

"Oh Lord, no. No sir. He don't gamble, either. The Lord don't need to gamble. He knows what is and He just passes His numbers on to me."

"Is that right?"

"Hand plow can't make furrows all by itself, Mister James. Lord knows that. So He just passes the numbers along, and it's like He is helpin' to push that hand plow along."

"Great mathematicians could have used His help, then."

"Don't know about that, don't know about that. The Lord has His own mysterious ways and gives His gifts to them that listen."

"And you listen?"

"Lord, yes," she said, and laughed. "Lord, yes. That I do, Mister James. I listen every night and every day for the numbers to come on down from Him."

"What's it going to be today?"

"What is what going to be?"

"The gift. The number."

"I can't go and tell you that."

"Why not?"

"Because, Mister James. It wouldn't be right."

"When will it be right, then?"

"When?"

"Yes, when?"

"When I'm ready for when," she told him, taking off her prized long black coat that had no winter lining. It was a coat she had bought in the secondhand store located behind her church. The lady who sold it had told her the coat's original owner had been none other than the private chauffeur for the Queen of England, and when the queen had visited Washington, D.C., she had brought along the chauffeur, who tragically had a heart attack soon after arriving. The coat somehow ended up in the church's secondhand store. The coat might as well have belonged to the queen herself as far as Jenniemae was concerned, and she proudly told anyone who would listen about the coat's history. It may not have been the warmest coat but it had the importance of class, which had its own warmth. The queen's chauffeur must have been a large person, since the coat was big even on Jenniemae and partly hid her size, something about which she was terribly ashamed. Jenniemae's weight was a burden. It limited her movement, it made her life constantly more difficult and painful, and it hid her real attractiveness. If it hadn't been for her weight, Jenniemae would have been considered a very attractive woman. She had a perfect complexion, with beautiful, smooth dark skin and naturally glowing cheeks. Her large dark brown eyes were made more striking by thick black brows and long eyelashes. Jenniemae's hair, which was long, black, and curly, was always neatly pulled back into a bun and rarely seen down, except by her nieces and nephews when she was brushing it out each night before bedtime. Jenniemae believed in things being neat and tidy—she routinely washed her hair every Sunday and Thursday— and kept her clothing spotlessly clean. When she arrived for work in the mornings, she would retreat to the small room located behind the kitchen. This was Jenniemae's room. It was commonly called the "maid's room," and it was here that Jenniemae kept her belongings. As soon as she arrived for work in the mornings, she would immediately change into her black- and-white uniform and hang her own clothes carefully in the closet.

"You don't have to be hangin' my coat," she chided my father as he carefully took it from her.

"Sure I do if I want that number."

"Never gonna happen. And you be careful with that coat, if you don't mind, Mister James. You be careful."

"I will. I will."

"You know I don't take to any man tryin' to smooth me over for no good reason."

"Why not?"

"Because there ain't never going to be a good thing when it's comin' from a bad-meanin' man."

"I'm not bad meaning. I just want to know what the number is."

"Oh, Lord have mercy. You never give up, do you, Mister James?"

"I don't see how you win all the time. How is it possible?"

"I got the dreams. It's all in the dreams. Simple thing. It's the Lord's way of givin' to me."

"You dream the numbers?"

"Yes indeed I do. The numbers are inside my dreams."

"There's a number hidden in a dream?"

"Always, Mister James. It's the Lord's gift and it floats on through the thin space-air and comes right into my dreams. And my guess is that those numbers are in other people's dreams, too, but they just don't be listenin' to them."

"Is that right?"

"It is, Mister James. A person has to listen to their own dreams and then they can see the numbers. Those numbers are there, but they just hidin' in the dream space."

"Really? Numbers in space."

"That's right. They are just waitin' to be seen."

"Maybe."

"Numbers are out there, Mister James. They are everywhere. Some of the times it is not an easy thing to see a number, but it is there no matter."

"Does every dream have a number attached to it?"

"Well, I can't say for everybody or every single dream. I can only say for my own dreams. And they are—every one of them—gifts from the Lord Himself. That ole river may be gone and muddy, and the creek may be bone and dry, but the Lord knows that if He gives gifts to His women, then His men won't go up and die."

"That's probably true, which is why I need your help here. Just one number," he tried.

"Can't be doin' it, Mister James. Can't be and since I got work

Brooke, 1949
*Author's collection*

to do here and I got a call to make, you best go on to your own work now."

"Is that right?"

"Yes sir, Mister James. And don't you forget that it's bad luck to be leavin' a chair rockin' when you get up."

"All right, I won't forget."

• • •

Both playing the daily numbers game and working with higher mathematics require a certain degree of obsessiveness. Both Jenniemae and James had obsessive personalities. Both of them liked order, routine, regularity; both were intense and rarely gave up on a subject once it was presented—which may have been why they weren't too concerned when they noticed some of the obsessive habits that I had developed by the age of four. I had begun to do what Jenniemae called "tappin'." I was a "tapper." Jenniemae called me a "tapper who was tappin' the music out of my head." I tapped doorknobs, tabletops, chairs, and bedposts. It was Jenniemae who first articulated what was going on with me. "You tappin', honey, aren't you?" she asked, and when I held my head low, she added, "Ain't nothin' to be ashamed about. Some people tap, some people hum, some people jump up and down or flap their hands around, and other people go and play with numbers. This is your very own special way of easin' into your day and makin' your life seem more settled. Isn't that right now?" I nodded in agreement.

"Nothin' to worry about. If you need to tap, then you go ahead and tap," she told me. So I did just that, and while I was busy tapping walls, knobs, and furniture, my father and Jenniemae were running numbers, either on paper or through the telephone lines. And because of their shared enjoyment of numbers and their shared wry sense of humor, a very special relationship was beginning to take hold.

# CHAPTER SIX

*"No use singin' spirituals to a dead mule."*

By the spring of 1949 the incoming morning telephone calls to the house were more often for Jenniemae than anyone else. Her friends telephoned to see if they could surreptitiously garner one of her dream numbers for that day. Her relatives called to warn her about giving away any family number secrets. And absolute strangers who had heard about this lucky woman with the magic policy touch called to plead or cajole that number out of her. The fact that no one ever succeeded in convincing Jenniemae to give up the number didn't seem to bother them. The calls continued no matter how insistent she was in her rejections. There were probably even bets placed on when Jenniemae Harrington might finally give up that lucky number. For her part, Jenniemae made a concerted effort to answer those calls after just one or two rings, but often that was impossible since she might be ironing or doing laundry in the basement or be caught elsewhere far away from the phone. And she made even more of a concerted effort to see that the telephone calls would not come in before my mother left for work. During these years my mother worked as a remedial-reading teacher in the D.C. schools (she had earned her master's degree in psychology from George Washington University in 1942), and though she was devoted to her work, she always had great difficulty getting up in the mornings and getting to work on time. She was a restless sleeper who dreaded the nights—she went to bed quite late (two or three in the morning was not uncommon) and almost always slept late, waiting until the last minute to finally rise and then quickly dress, put on her makeup, and rush downstairs to the kitchen, where, standing, she would gulp down her two or three cups of coffee while smoking her first cigarette of the day. To say that she was on edge and impatient would be a gross understatement. We all avoided her if possible in the morning, and the ringing of the telephone before she left for work would have been a precarious annoyance—one about which Jenniemae was well aware.

If Jenniemae was not nearby, it was my father who answered the calls, even if my mother was home.

"Hello."

"Is there a J-mae there, please?"

"Jenniemae?"

"Yes sir. J-mae. Is she there?"

"Well, hold on a minute. . . . Jenniemae, the phone's for you," he would call downstairs.

"Oh Lord," she would call up. "Me?"

"I believe so, Jenniemae. It's for you."

"Mister James . . . just please hold on a little bit while I get up there. Just hold on and thank the Lord for me to make it there without dyin' by tryin'. Lord have mercy."

"Take your time. Take your time . . . no one is going anywhere . . . but don't be giving out any family secrets while you're on the phone."

Jenniemae almost always reprimanded the callers and did her best to get off the telephone quickly. She would then apologize to my father for the inconvenience and promise to try her best to make the calls stop. But that seemed an impossibility, which is when my father decided to solve the problem—and along the way endear himself to her with the hope of retrieving that magic number.

One evening while we were having supper, he announced that he was having a new telephone line installed in the house. We were—my father, mother, brother, and me—sitting around the maple dining-room table that always was dressed at mealtimes with an ironed linen tablecloth and ironed linen napkins. A silver bell sat in the middle of the table and, when necessary, was given a slight shake by my mother to announce to Jenniemae when one course was finished and another should be served. Silver monogrammed salt and pepper shakers sat alongside a silver monogrammed butter dish. Supper was always a formal affair and we dressed for the occasion. My mother and I wore dresses or a skirt and blouse, my brother wore khakis and a button-down shirt, and my father wore a three-piece suit and tie. Conversations were usually between my parents unless either my brother or I were asked a question. At the end of the meal we were expected to ask permission to be excused to leave the table. Jenniemae, who always wore a freshly ironed black-and-white dress, served us four courses: soup, a main course, salad, and dessert. However, as formal as the serving and attire was, my parents' conversations frequently were not so refined.

"We're going to be getting a second telephone line installed in the house," my father told us that day.

"And why is that?" My mother stared at him with the usual frustration and irritation in her eyes.

"Because it is," he said sternly, staring back across the table with his steely blue eyes.

"You have to have a second line? One isn't enough?"

"No."

"I don't understand why a second line is necessary," she said.

"Because it simply is."

"It simply is?" She repeated his words.

"That's how I see it."

"Well, explain to me what the need is."

"I don't need it. Jenniemae needs it," he announced.

"What?"

"That's right."

"You're not serious?"

"Oh, but I am."

"And is she paying for it?"

"Don't be ridiculous."

"Ridiculous? You think I'm being ridiculous?"

"This is not open for discussion."

"Is that right?"

"Yes, that's right. The line is being put in and that's that."

My brother and I would watch these frequent arguments the same way people might watch a tennis match—quietly following the back-and-forth volley of words but never intervening. Arguments between my parents generally began or ended by virtue of my father's say-so, and no one expected otherwise. My mother tried to stand her ground and she was clear about what might be considered unacceptable. Stepping over the edge might have entailed slamming silverware onto the plates, yelling loudly, leaving the table in a huff, and/or crying. My own vivid recollection of that dinner-table scene had more to do with the excitement of getting a new phone than anything else. The idea that we would have two different lines with two different telephone numbers in our house was a novelty even though this new line would not be one I would ever use. In 1949 no one, I imagined, except maybe the president of the United States or J. Edgar Hoover, the head of the FBI, had more than one telephone line.

Within days, the telephone man arrived. It was late in the afternoon. The front doorbell rang and my father, dressed as usual in a three-piece suit, bow tie, and shined black shoes, went to answer it. I watched from the stairwell as he greeted the telephone serviceman. It was always exciting to watch something new in the house, and despite my nervous tics, I liked change. I wasn't a child who wanted everything to remain in the same place or have every event unfold at the same time each day. I looked forward to new things and new events. If I had been a snake, I would have looked forward to shedding my old skin and growing a new one every year. My life at five was already filled with enough tension to last a lifetime. I feared that my father would die at any moment. I feared that my mother's night terrors might transform her into someone we couldn't control and that she might do something terrible. It was not unusual for her during one of these episodes to come into my bedroom, which was across the hall from her own (it was explained that my parents did not share a bedroom because of the night terrors), and then crawl into my small bed. Was she sleeping? Was she awake? Was she my mother? Had she transformed into someone else? It never took long—at least in my recollection of these events—before she would begin to flail her arms and kick her feet, sending me onto the floor. It was also not at all unusual that I would then retreat into the closet, where I would spend the rest of the night hours huddled. It was also not unusual for me to wake in the morning in my closet, my mother having already returned to her own bedroom, probably completely unaware of where she had been during the night or what she had done. As peculiar or haunting as this may seem, it was also what I had become accustomed to at an early age, which is not to say that I wasn't affected by it all—because I most certainly was—but it was what I knew. Remaining quiet about these times was another thing I knew to do and assumed was expected of me. No one asked and no one told. It just was what it was. And one of the consequences of this, and the complex relationship my mother and I developed, was that there were so many skeletons continually amassing in the closet, neither one of us knew where to begin unlocking secrets. There was an unsettling and tacit understanding that opening that closet door might uncover such a mess of bones, such a tangled cluster, that it was better to keep the door closed. And that is what we did. My mother and I frequently went about our ways in denial. From a very young age I cultivated—sometimes consciously and other times not—an emotional distance from my mother which became more difficult to penetrate as the years went on. Without question I loved her—and she me—but I would always feel a bit suspect, would always feel an edge of distrust. I looked to my father for support, advice, and confidence far more often than I ever did my mother. When in doubt, my questions were directed toward him—and he almost always had an answer. I simply would not have considered going to my mother the way my brother might have—it just was the peculiar mix of our family.

I feared both my father's and my mother's seesaw battles with depression and that my mother's dark depressions would one day take her over the edge to a hospital (a possibility I recall being discussed by my father and doctors on the telephone). Fortunately, there was always Jenniemae to bring reason and humor into my days and to take my mind off these possibilities. Though I doubt Jenniemae had any idea about my mother's night terrors, she was well aware that there were disquieting tensions in the house that seemed to put an extra burden on my soul and that I was a child who found distractions a relief. Change was something I prayed for, and when the telephone man arrived to put a second line in the house, I was thrilled.

"Hello," my father said as he opened the front door.

"I have an order to put a second line in your house. Is this the right house?"

"Yes, indeed. Come right in."

"Where would you like the line? Office?" The telephone repairman was all business.

"No, not exactly."

"Oh? Where, then?"

"Well, why don't you just step inside and I'll show you," my father suggested, stepping aside to allow him into the house. A round mahogany table stood in the center of the entryway. Upon it was a hand-painted eighteenth-century Russian vase. The carpet was a plush Persian carpet with red and blue threads tightly woven into an ancient floral pattern.

"Should I remove my shoes?"

"No need."

The repairman carried a black case filled with tools and a new black rotary-dial telephone. "Where exactly would you like the phone?"

My father motioned for the man to follow, which he did, and I quietly followed the two of them through the entryway, the dining area, the kitchen, and then down another short hallway to Jenniemae's back room. The rectangular room was only large enough for one bed, a closet, an antique sewing table, and a rocking chair.

The pale-white, forty-something telephone man, who was neatly dressed in dark-blue company pants and a white company shirt with a C&P (Chesapeake and Potomac) Telephone Company logo on the pocket, looked around the small room.

"Here is where I want it," my father said, pointing to the wall next to the sewing table.

The phone man didn't say a word.

My father repeated, "Right there. On that table would be fine."

The telephone man looked stunned. "Do you understand?" my father asked.

The man stared at my father and then shifted his weight from one foot to the other. He again looked around the room. "Back here?"

"Yes, that's correct."

"Really?"

"Yes, a telephone back in this room here."

"Sir."

"Yes?"

"Is this a joke?"

"No. No, it's not a joke. I want the telephone installed in this room."

It was then that the phone man made the mistake of saying, "Why in the hell would anyone want a line put back here where the nigger is living?"

"Oh, I don't know. Perhaps she might want to make some calls."

"What?"

"That's what I said," my father barked as he left the room.

"Well, that's your own waste of money. A phone for a nigger . . . beats me."

This was the first time I had ever heard the word *nigger*. At the age of five the word itself didn't mean anything, but the way it was said did. *Nigger* was clearly a bad word to be called and a sorry thing to be. *Nigger* was what the telephone man had called Jenniemae, whom I already loved. I also was aware that she was not "one of us." She was overweight, she cooked and cleaned the house, she took care of my brother and me, and her skin was dark brown. Now she was called a "nigger," and from the way it rolled like spit out of the telephone man's mouth, it clearly was not a good word.

Jenniemae had been in the basement during the installation of the telephone and had no idea what was going on. When the phone man finally left the house and a black telephone could be seen sitting in the middle of a small antique sewing table, James, ever impatient, could not wait to show her the new toy he had purchased.

"Jenniemae?" he called out.

Jenniemae must have suspected something was going on upstairs—just a second sense—and not trusting Mister James's sometimes unpredictable behavior, she had stayed away. "I have work to do down here, Mister James," she answered.

"Could you please just leave it for a moment and come up . . . if you don't mind."

"Now, if I go an' leave things all the time jus' cause the wind blows this way or that, then I be here all night long ironin' these here shirts of yours."

"Jenniemae, just for a moment."

"I ain't got a moment to spare, Mister James. I got a burning-hot iron down here."

"Forget the damn shirts," he said, frustrated.

"Now, Mister James, that ain't no way to be talkin'."

"Jenniemae, please."

"Okay now, okay. Lord have mercy. You jus' be holdin' on 'cause I got to put this hot iron away before it burns a hole in these here shirts. I ain't some young chicken here, you know," she said, turning the iron off and pulling the plug out of the wall socket, which was something she always did, never trusting that just because a thing was turned off, it was off. It was her belief that the electricity would just keep coming through the walls and possibly burn the entire house down, no matter whether a person turned a thing to an off position or not.

Slowly Jenniemae made it to the landing, where my father was impatiently waiting.

"About time," he said. "I have something to show you, so if you would be kind enough to follow me back here, then I can get back to my work also."

"I got my work, too. You think I can jus' take time to climb these here stairs whenever you want?"

"You're almost as difficult as my wife. Almost."

"Lord, Mister James, you are a hard man," she said as she followed my father down the hallway, then through the kitchen to her back room.

My father smiled as he proudly walked over to the antique sewing table and pointed to the black rotary-dial telephone.

"What is that?" Jenniemae said as if she didn't know exactly what it was.

"That is your personal and private phone," he said proudly.

Jenniemae was quiet. She looked toward my father, glanced toward me, and then stared at the telephone.

"What do you think?" he asked her proudly.

"Well, Lord have mercy. My oh my . . . but jus' what am I s'posed to do with it?"

"What you always do with a phone."

"But back here?"

"Why not?"

"Why not?"

"Yes, why not back here?"

"What do you mean, why not?"

"Just what I said, Jenniemae. It's your own phone."

"My phone?"

"Yes, your phone."

"But . . ."

James continued, "You have your own telephone number."

"What? Oh, Lord have mercy, no."

"Yes. Yes you do," he told her.

"What kind of number?"

"What kind?"

"What kind of number is it?" She was nervous.

"It's a good number. It's your own number," he assured her.

"Now, what in the Lord's name . . . I mean what am I goin' to be doin' with my own number?" she said, flustered.

"What do you mean, what? You will have this line to make your own calls every morning and then people can call you back. On your own line here."

"My own number line?"

"Yes indeed. Your own number line."

"My Lord. Oh Lord."

"Well, maybe you shouldn't be thanking some Lord, seeing as how most of your calls have to do with gambling."

"It's not gambling."

"Oh, really! Then what exactly is it?"

"It is dream numbers. Dream numbers are gifts to be given by the Lord Himself."

"Well, whatever it is . . . you can call in the numbers in private on your own line now. Of course, if you wish to share those numbers anytime with me . . . feel free. Now I have got to be getting back to work."

Jenniemae smiled as he walked out of the room. She said softly, "Thanks to you, Mister James. I never had a gift like this before. With a number in it, too. Thanks to you. But I'm not doin' any sharin' of my dream numbers." Then Jenniemae walked over to the black rotary phone, stared at it for a moment, then picked up the receiver and listened to the dial tone. "Oh Lord. Oh Lord."

When my father left the room, Jenniemae sat down next to the telephone and stared at it. "Come on over here, child, and look at this here thing." She motioned to me to sit on her lap. "Look here now. It's our telephone. And this phone has got its own number. Lord have mercy for that, child. Now, you touch it first 'cause I got a feelin' that if you touch it first, then everything will be all right. You hear me now. Everything will be all right. So you go ahead and touch it first." She smiled and lifted my hand and I tapped the receiver twice.

"It's nice and smooth now, isn't it? And soon you will see that you only are needin' to be touchin' this phone once 'cause it's gonna give you the luck to not have a need for tappin' a thing more than one time," she told me.

"Really?"

"Yes, I promise it."

And so I lifted my hand up and again put it down to touch Jenniemae's phone just once. But I had to tap it twice.

"Don't you worry, you'll get there," Jenniemae said, probably hoping that I would be able to conquer the tapping habit that she could not overcome in her own life.

"It's really a smooth phone. You touch it," I told her.

"Okay then, I will," she said as she ran her fingers over the back of the receiver. "We'll make us some calls here."

"Now?" I asked.

"I don't know about now. The telephone needs its rest now. Can't be jus' usin' it any ole time. It needs to get settled into its new home here. Right?"

"Right," I agreed.

"Everything has its own way of settling in to a new place. Right now this here phone looks to be uncomfortable because it hasn't settled, but if we give it a few days—maybe even a week or more—it will make itself at home and look like it could have been right here for years."

And, of course, Jenniemae was right about that. For the first few days the black telephone looked out of place on the table in her back room, but after a couple of weeks it looked as if it belonged there just as much as everything else that had settled into the room.

# CHAPTER SEVEN

*"Dog don't be gettin' mad when you say he's a dog."*

The installation of that second line was a major event in our house. For Jenniemae the gift had more value than a diamond necklace. She was the proud owner of a black rotary-dial telephone, and no matter what others might have thought or said to the contrary, she believed the telephone had both a mind and a heartbeat of its own. So she cared for it with proper respect: She dusted and cleaned it carefully every single morning, she checked the health of the dial tone frequently during the day, she made certain it stayed in the middle of the table so it couldn't possibly fall off while ringing, and she checked that the line was clear of debris. "It's not gonna ring right if it isn't cared for right," she said. "A phone knows what a phone knows, and this here phone knows more than most."

My mother, however, was not as pleased with the arrival of the telephone. It was not that she was against helping Jenniemae out, or anyone who worked for her; rather, it was that she felt uncomfortable forging a relationship with "hired help."

My mother was a woman who had grown up with fairly formal attitudes—her mother had been a proper Southern Louisiana lady, and it wasn't as if interacting with the "maid" was particularly distasteful, it was just unheard of. If she had ever been asked how she felt about Jenniemae, she probably would have responded that she liked her and thought she did her job well. But she was not like her husband, who found it easy to have a conversation with the maid or the gardener or the garbageman. She wanted a hands-off relationship with Jenniemae, and any more than that would have been uncomfortable for her. And when it came to the new telephone, although she hadn't been home during the installation, she knew as soon as she walked into the house that the telephone man had come and gone and a second line had been put in place. Jenniemae was keenly aware that my mother did not approve of the phone and was careful not to mention it in her pressence, but my mother was no fool, and she was aware of many of the things that went on in her house when she wasn't around. I believe my mother initially did her best to block it out of her mind. But the telephone was sort of an elephant in the house, and after a week or so it seemed to take on a life of its own. As far as my mother was concerned, it was there but it wasn't there.

For the first couple of weeks the phone never rang when my mother was home. How it knew not to ring was anyone's guess. Jenniemae would have said that the telephone was just getting used to the room and needed its rest, but obviously it had something to do with Jenniemae's insistence and lectures to her friends and family that they not call her number. It took at least two weeks before it ever did ring—and even then it would rarely ring in the mornings before my mother's car had completely disappeared down the road and past the stop sign at the corner.

However, that telephone was there—it existed in her house—and no matter its silence before she left for work, my mother could not block the telephone's presence from her mind and go on with her life as usual. She couldn't help but be angry over its presence in her house. It was there, in her house, and in the back maid's room. She considered that perhaps if she refused to acknowledge its actuality by never once going to the back room, if she never set eyes on it, then maybe it would soon cease to exist or, at the very least, it would no longer bother her. That theory failed to work, however, and one night after Jenniemae had gone home and the rest of the family had gone to bed, she decided to confront the issue by going in to look at the phone. It is strange how an inanimate thing can change lives. It doesn't breathe or think, make choices or judgments, and yet all of a sudden that thing becomes animate and demands attention.

Even the dogs were sleeping soundly when my mother tiptoed down the stairs, walked through the kitchen and into the back room just to have a look at the telephone. And there it was. The Phone. Immediately she noticed that the telephone had been set on a small cherry antique sewing table that used to stand in the front entryway, the very same antique cherry sewing table with hand-painted flowers twining around the legs that once belonged to her mother (and now sits in my living room). I am certain that my mother must have hissed profanities seeing her mother's antique sewing table abused in this way. I wasn't there, but it was obvious from what we saw the next morning that she must have been furious, because she then proceeded to spend the next several hours moving furniture around the house. It wasn't simply that the telephone had to be moved—it was that everything had to be rearranged. Her house had been tampered with and she had to repair the rift.

It started with the antique table but went on from there. Tables and chairs were moved from one room to another. Paintings were taken down and hung on different walls. Carpets were rolled up and dragged across floors. Decorative vases were transferred from one countertop to another. She even rearranged the china in the cabinets. This redecorating kept my mother up most of the night. Beyond the overall effect of our awakening to a newly designed home, there was the added fact that the antique sewing table was now in my mother's bedroom, and in Jenniemae's back room, the black telephone now rested on a small maple chest with ornate brass knobs that had been in my father's mother's family for at least two generations. And when my father complained about the rearrangement of furniture, my mother simply said, "Let the maid's phone rest on your mother's soul."

Naturally, Jenniemae noticed the changes as soon as she walked through the door in the morning. Rather than cause any conflict, she chose to compliment my mother on the new way the house looked, and she even thanked her: "I do appreciate the new table you put in my room, Missus Ruth. I do appreciate it. Thank you so very much."

To which my mother replied, "Oh, why, it was . . . nothing."

"Oh no, Missus Ruth, I am certain it was something, and I appreciate your taking the time to help my room out with a fine-lookin' table."

"Well, that's nice. Enjoy it." My mother nodded her head and smiled before leaving for work.

Soon after she had walked out the door, Jenniemae reprimanded James. "Now, Mister James, you have to leave these tables and chairs where Missus Ruth put them so she can breathe some. It ain't worth the problem it causes you two. You hear me? It ain't gonna be doin' you nor me any good if you start in on movin' things that are in the upstairs to the downstairs and things that are in the downstairs gettin' on moved to the upstairs. It is best to let Missus Ruth put tables and such where she wants them to be. You don't need to go and cause her to be riled up about any of this. You hear me?"

He listened and smiled. "You take the fun out of being married."

"Oh, Lord, you are more trouble than it's worth."

"No, I'm not. I am worth more trouble than you have got to give."

"You jus' keep thinking like that, Mister James, and you gonna get yo'self in a whole heap of trouble every day." She shook her head as she left the room.

For all the trouble it caused at the start, you would have thought the telephone would have been put to use right away, but that wasn't the case. As mentioned, during the first fourteen days the telephone rested, and then by day fifteen or sixteen Jenniemae told me, "It is time." When I asked, "Time for what?"

she replied that it was time for the telephone to do what it was meant to do and get to work. I watched as she made her own first outgoing telephone call to her sister.

"It's me, honey," Jenniemae said quickly, as if the line would only allow her but a second to speak.

"You who?" her sister said.

"Me. It's me here an' talkin' to you on my own, very own, black phone."

"Best be black, honey. Best be black." Jenniemae's sister laughed.

"What is that s'posed to mean?"

"You jus' remember who you are when you be dialin' away on that phone," she advised Jenniemae.

"What are you meaning?"

"I am meaning that you jus' has to remember to keep your place."

"I know my place," Jenniemae insisted.

"Do you now?"

"Yes I do."

"Dog don't be gettin' mad when you say he's a dog," Jenniemae's sister said.

"You sayin' I'm a dog?"

"I'm sayin' you know what I'm sayin'," her sister returned.

"And I'm sayin' you jus' jealous you don't have a nice new phone."

"Well, ain't that a fact!" she said, and laughed.

And they both started laughing.

It didn't take long after this first call for Jenniemae to find that black telephone extraordinarily useful. She made her daily calls to the man but rarely made any other calls. As time went on and she continued to win her bets, the phone rang more often; even absolute strangers discovered her telephone number. Every caller wanted one thing and one thing only: for Jenniemae to reveal her daily number. But that never happened.

# CHAPTER EIGHT

*"Old Used-to-Do-It-This-Way don't help none today."*

A few weeks before Christmas that year, Jenniemae came down with a high fever and a wicked, rumbling cough that settled deep in her chest. My mother hated to have sick people in the house, fearing that once you let a disease in the front door, it was likely to overtake the entire household. To some degree it would be hard to blame her for feeling this way, since in 1949 more than 42,000 cases of polio had been reported and more than 2,500 people had died from it. There was a "polio panic" in the United States and few people didn't worry. However, for my mother the sign of any disease in the house—whether polio or the common cold—was a sign of impending danger. Perhaps because she was a working mother who wasn't home taking care of her children, she was far more apprehensive about strange illnesses entering our lives than she might have been otherwise. I don't know that she ever felt particularly guilty about working, but she would have been completely miffed if anyone were to suggest that she should stay home to care for one of her children if they got sick. Germs came under the heading of the many dangers that might disrupt her fragile balance, so to guard against any calamity, my mother protected her house in every possible way—and staying away from sick people was obviously at the top of the list of potential perils.

However, the illness that overtook Jenniemae came on without the usual warning signs. One day Jenniemae seemed perfectly healthy and the next she had a high fever and a rough cough. By the time she arrived at work, her temperature had climbed to 104 degrees. Clearly she was too sick and weak either to work or to go home, so my mother had no choice but to ask her to stay in the back room until she felt better. Though I was only a small child, I was old enough to understand that diseases could spread, and also old enough to get in trouble while wandering through the house alone, so my mother asked that I keep a distant eye— as distant as possible, she suggested—on Jenniemae every so often, believing that this might keep me occupied.

"Just look in on her, sweetheart. Don't go inside the room— just open the door, and if she's not sleeping, then ask her if she is okay. That's all you should do. But do not touch her. No matter what—do not touch her. You know how a cough can spread from one person to another, and the next thing you know, you could end up in the hospital."

"Hospital?"

"Absolutely. The combination of a cough and a high fever is a very dangerous signal. Very dangerous. So you must stay away from Jenniemae."

"Is Dr. Schwartz coming to see her?" I asked.

"No, no. He won't be coming."

"Why not? Jenniemae is sick."

"She'll get better without our doctor. And she probably has her own doctor in her neighborhood. It is better if she keeps to her own doctor," my mother said before leaving.

As soon as I could hear my mother's car door shut and the engine start, I went into Jenniemae's room to check on her.

"You not s'posed to be in here, child," Jenniemae said, looking up from the pillow. Her dark brown skin looked yellow and her eyes were swollen.

"I know. But I'm already here."

"I can see that." She tried to smile.

"What's the matter with you?"

"Oh, child, I got the fever and the cough. You need to stay far away from me so as not to get it."

"I won't get it."

"You jus' might."

"No, I promise I won't."

"But if you do your mama will be mighty mad."

"I won't get sick. I promise I won't."

"I appreciate that but, child, you can't promise something you don't have control on. And Lord knows you can't get sick before Jesus' birthday, honey."

"Why?"

"Because it's a fine day to celebrate and you don't want to be sick."

"But you're sick. Does Jesus know you're sick?"

"He knows and I pray He'll be there to make me healthy again."

"Is Jesus a doctor?"

"Better than most doctors."

"Better than Dr. Schwartz?"

She began to cough—spasms of coughing caused her to double over in bed. "Oh Lord. Oh Lord," she repeated between coughing fits. I stood next to the bed, holding out her glass of water, which she took sips from whenever she could without coughing and spilling. "Thank you, honey. Thank the Lord and thank you," she said, coughing.

"Maybe Jesus better come soon, huh?"

"Maybe, child, maybe."

Every time the coughing started up again, I thought Jenniemae might stop breathing. I was terribly worried. When finally she fell into a deep sleep, I stood beside the bed and watched her breathe, fearful that she might die if I didn't keep my eye on her. I didn't have much of an idea how a prayer might be said since my parents were Jewish atheists and scoffed at any religious practices. Christmas was for the tree, the lights, and the presents; Easter was for dyeing eggs; Passover was for gathering friends together and drinking cheap wine, and Yom Kippur and Rosh Hashanah were never observed in our house. But I surely wanted to say some silent something to someone somewhere to plead my case for Jenniemae to get better. The only form of prayer I could come up with, I said in a quiet whisper:

"Star light, star bright, first star I see tonight (or this morning), I wish I may, I wish I might, have this wish I wish tonight . . . I wish that Jenniemae gets better soon."

Jenniemae slept most of the morning, only stirring to cough. During each of those episodes I repeated my wish. By midafternoon Jenniemae's coloring seemed to have changed from a yellow hue to a red one. Sweat appeared across her forehead and cheeks and tiny beads of it dripped into her hair. Every once in a while she would open her reddened eyes, look toward me, and attempt to smile. Then her eyes would close again and she would fall back into a deep sleep. I sat beside the bed and watched her breathing, and when beads of sweat formed, I lay my sleeve across her forehead to wipe it dry. At one point she awoke with a start, sat up and cried out, "No, no," and then began another coughing fit. I thought she might be dying.

"Are you going to die, Jenniemae?" She stared at me, trying to focus on why I was there and what I was asking. After a few moments she seemed to figure out what I had asked. "Oh Lord . . . die . . . no, child. Not now. No, honey, I'll be okay jus' soon as I break the fever."

"Are you sure? Maybe you should use the telephone to call Dr. Schwartz."

"No, child, I'll be all right. The good Lord don't want me yet and the good doctor isn't gonna come. I'll be better by nightfall, and as soon as I get to my home, my sister can take good care of me."

I was relieved that Jenniemae wasn't going to die but also considered it strange that she could have such a close connection with the Lord but she couldn't have a connection with Dr. Schwartz.

"You're going home?"

"As soon as I can stand on my own two feet, honey, I am takin' that bus home."

"But—"

"Child, I'll be better sleepin' in my own bed and seein' my own kind of doctor," Jenniemae said. Sure enough, a few hours later, before my mother arrived home, Jenniemae struggled up, dragged herself out of the house, and headed up the block to the bus stop. Before she left she told me to tell my mother how sorry she was for not being able to get her work done and get the dinner prepared. "You be sure and tell her that now, okay, honey child?" she said between coughing fits.

"Yes, I will," I promised.

When my mother got home, I did tell her that Jenniemae was sorry for not cleaning the house and cooking the supper. My mother smiled and simply asked, "Did you stay away from her, though?" I told her I did.

Three days later I came down with a high fever and a cough. My mother wanted to fire Jenniemae but that was out of the question.

"She made her sick. Can't you see that?" she said to my father.

"You don't know that, and even if it's so, it doesn't matter. That's life."

"That's not my life."

"It is now."

That night my fever spiked to 105, and just before midnight Dr. Schwartz arrived. I was delirious, but I do recall telling him that I was glad he was there but I wondered if he could ask the Lord to come also. Dr. Schwartz laughed. I slept on and off for three days. Jenniemae was feeling better by then and took care of me, putting cool cloths on my forehead and changing my drenched sheets often. I asked her if the Lord was going to come and make me better. She said that He would. She also reminded me that it was close to Christmas and the birthday of Jesus Christ, His son, so it was important for me to be better before that day. But I didn't get better, and spent Christmas Eve and Christmas Day in bed. To console me, my brother brought his and my gifts into the bedroom, opened them all, and described each one as I lay listlessly in bed. My mother brought cool cloths for my forehead and later in the day she cooked a special meal. While she cooked, my father sat beside my bed.

"Your mother is making you a special supper," he told me.

"But I don't like the green drink," I told him. There was a green concoction my mother made that consisted of squeezed spinach juice, herbs, and lemon that she swore by when we became ill. It tasted horrible.

"I know, but you always find a way to get through it," he said, smiling. He was fully aware of my habit of pouring the drink down the sink as soon as my mother left the room.

"Have you ever tried it?" I asked him.

"She knows better than to ask me."

"Aren't you afraid that if you sit with me you will get sick?"

"No. I won't get sick," he told me. But four days later he, too, came down with the high fever and cough. I recovered before New Year's Eve, but my father remained in bed. He stayed in bed that day and the next—and for the next ten weeks. His fever went up and down like a roller coaster, and his cough came on in long, harsh spasms. My father became sicker than Jenniemae or me, until what he had turned into pneumonia. Dr. Schwartz came every day for weeks.

"Is he going to die?" I asked Jenniemae one afternoon.

"No, child. He'll be fine."

"But he's been sick a long time."

"Some people need more time than others," she reassured me, but I wasn't sure.

"I gave it to him . . . and he might die."

"No, child. He just needs time. You go and sit by him. That's gonna make him feel better more than the doctor comin'."

So every day I sat on the corner of my father's bed. He slept for the better part of the days. Jenniemae prayed for him to get stronger and I watched and studied her praying, thinking that one day those prayers might come in handy. Well into the second month of my father's pneumonia, his temperature finally dropped below 100 degrees. Both my mother and Jenniemae said that was a good milestone. His current girlfriend, who wasn't living with us—yet—also visited, much to Jenniemae's annoyance.

"She shouldn't be here, Mister James. That's no way to get back on your feet, havin' some street lady like that show up." She was always direct about his girlfriends.

"She's nice."

"No, she's not nice, and next time she comes I'm gonna tell her to leave."

"Don't do that."

"Oh, I sure will do that," she insisted. He knew better than to argue.

The girlfriend didn't come again until my father was over his pneumonia. Soon after his temperature dropped, my father began to feel better though he was still bedridden and napped on and off during each day. The first true sign of his returning strength came a week or so after his temperature had leveled off. One afternoon he propped himself up with pillows, put a wooden chess set on his lap, and began to play. I sat at the end of his bed and watched. Sometimes he would mumble to himself or grin as he made a move with a chess piece. After watching for a few days, I asked if he would teach me how to play.

My father was a gentle and patient teacher, showing me how each piece moved and explaining the point of the game. I listened as best I could but mostly I loved the smooth feel and weight of the heavy chess pieces, particularly the king and queen, which stood taller than the others. My favorite two pieces, however, were the knights—the handsome horses—and every chance I got, I played a knight.

"You can't win with the knight alone," he told me.

"But I have two knights."

"More reason to be sparing."

"Please don't take my knight, then."

"You can't ask your opponent not to take a piece."

"Why not?"

"Because that's not how the game is played. You have to figure out how to protect the knight if you don't want him taken."

Every morning after his breakfast tea and muffin, my father patiently played a child's version of chess with me. At one point he suggested that Jenniemae could also learn to play. When she laughed at this, he insisted, "You could."

"Lord, no, Mister James. Lord, no."

"Yes you could."

"And even if I could, I have no need and no time for it."

"You would like it."

"No sir, Mister James. I can't be takin' the time with games."

"It's like playing the numbers," he said. "You make a move and take a chance."

"No, it's not like that one bit. My numbers aren't like pieces on some wooden board."

"Come on now. It's just a game."

"Lord have mercy no, Mister James. I'll jus' watch."

And since he knew there was a limit to how far he could push Jenniemae, he backed off. But frequently he would make chess moves—alone or against me—and describe them out loud, as if trying to teach Jenniemae without admitting to it, and she caught on quickly.

"The king can only move one square this way or that way," he would say, "though there is an exception to the king's moves and that is when he is castling, which means the king moves two squares toward the rook and the rook moves on the far side of the king. Then the queen—"

"I'm not gonna listen to this, so no use sayin' it out loud, Mister James."

"I'm just speaking out loud to myself."

"No, you're jus' tryin' to fill my head with information I ain't got no use with."

"Everyone's got use for a game."

"I got my own games."

"Like what?" he asked, surprised.

"Like games I play. My games."

"What are they?" he inquired.

"I play the card games with my sister and my friend John-John."

"Really?"

"You don't think we have our own card games?"

"Well, no, I guess . . ."

"Well, we do. Some the same as your own and some different," she explained.

"I never thought about it really."

"Sure 'nough you didn't. My people got games. We got games with cards and counting number cards," she said proudly.

"Show me one of them."

"One of my card games?"

"Sure," he said, and after locating two decks of cards, Jenniemae showed him a game. "It's like casino," he told her.

"Don't know about that because we call it sumbo."

"Really? Well, it's like what I call casino. You match suits and add numbers to win different hands—like casino."

"Then we got another game we call kalookie. We play that when there is a party of folks." And she explained kalookie, which my father said was a lot like rummy.

"People say the games are right out of the Good Book," she said, "and I chose to believe that to be the truth."

"I knew the Lord had to be a gambler."

"Not a gambler, Mister James. He's not a gambler. But maybe He's a game player, which is why He likes to watch His people move about."

It took my father over two months to recover, but considering that I learned how to play chess and Jenniemae taught my father sumbo and kalookie and he taught her casino, it wasn't time spent badly. And while playing cards—particularly casino, which requires the ability to add and subtract—it became clear that Jenniemae was quite able with numbers. My father wasn't really surprised. She allowed as to how numbers had always come easily to her since it was something a person lived with every day no matter if it had to do with sewing, cooking, or planting rows of vegetables in the garden.

"I may not know my reading words, but numbers are something every person wakes up and lives with all day long," she said, which was music to his ears.

"You're a natural," he told her.

There were days when Jenniemae suggested that my father wasn't trying to get better, because he had most everything he wanted right there in that room. He ate his meals in bed, read his books, had paper and pens close at hand, had the telephone on the table beside him, and had two women to talk to and play games with.

# CHAPTER NINE

*"Buzzard ain't circlin' in the air jus' for fun."*

The 1950s rolled in. Because the country was tired of war, weapons, and discontent, it seemed as if the fifties might be the decade for complacency. But not for long. Fear and paranoia undermined any sense of calm in the nation. The United States soon found itself at war again, this time in Korea. The Korean War, which began in June of 1950 and lasted until July of 1953, cost the United States more than 36,000 lives, the Chinese approximately 400,000, and the Koreans (both North and South) approximately 2 million. Once again the idea of using the atomic bomb during warfare was discussed, leading to intense protests and pressure by United Nations allies against such a drastic measure, and ultimately to the firing of General MacArthur. The impossibility of a simple resolution regarding how leaders of countries would deal with atomic power during times of war was resurfacing—as this issue would for years to come. The notion that peace would last for more than a moment around the world—and would not involve the United States—was a dream, pure delusion. Just because the country was tired of war didn't mean it wouldn't engage in another one. Later in the decade the United States would give the French $750 million to aid in their war against the Communists in Vietnam—and soon the United States would get involved there as well, and the war would escalate. The 1950s was a decade of turmoil, not complacency. War and weapons of mass destruction were occupying the minds and taking over the discourse of those around the country. In Washington, D.C., this was particularly true. Heated arguments arose between members of Congress, the military, and involved scientists about whether or not to move forward in building a potentially world-destroying hydrogen bomb—the Super, as it was called. The Super was the bomb to end all bombs, the ultimate weapon of darkness—the apocalypse. Exploding a hydrogen bomb was not like exploding an atomic bomb—as horrible as that was in itself—it was like exploding five hundred atomic bombs. In Winston Churchill's last speech to the House of Commons on March 1, 1955, he stated, "There is an immense gulf between the atomic and the hydrogen bomb. The atomic bomb, with all its terrors, did not carry us outside the scope of human control or manageable events in thought or action, in peace or war."

With war again preoccupying the nation and a growing fear of potential nuclear destruction on the horizon, alongside a growing apprehension that the Soviet Union would soon develop a hydrogen bomb, it was almost inevitable that the country would be enveloped in a thick cloud of distrust. By August of 1949 the Russians had blockaded Berlin and turned

Poland and Eastern Europe into Communist regimes. All people and things "Communist" became feared, hated, and hunted. Seizing on this sense of fear was the senator from Wisconsin Joseph McCarthy. McCarthy stepped forward to capitalize on the country's apprehensiveness, claiming that dangerous spies and Communists and Communist sympathizers were possibly— and probably—any- and everywhere in the United States and that they had to be uncovered and exposed. The Army-McCarthy hearings got under way and Americans paid close attention, listening to them on the radio, reading about them in the newspapers, and watching them on television.

Schools commonly held air-raid drills, which no child could easily forget. In elementary school I recall being told that it was required we follow a procedure called "Duck and Cover." "Duck and Cover" meant that as soon as the air-raid siren sounded, we were to quickly push back our chairs, throw ourselves onto the floor, hide under our desks, and duck from any potential flying debris. The school principal also suggested that the children wear identification tags so that our bodies could be identified should that be necessary. The idea that "Duck and Cover" might be a ludicrous waste of time, since no one would survive should a bomb be dropped on or near our school, was completely dismissed. And my father, who was never one to mince words or whitewash an issue, was infuriated that the schools would suggest that doing these drills might save any child's life. This, of course, did not help calm or mitigate my multiple fears. I dutifully followed all the air-raid procedures, hoping that my father might be wrong, while knowing that if—and when—that bomb was dropped from the blue sky above, I would most likely be incinerated alongside my classmates. These were not easy times to be a student in school.

On June 19, 1953, Ethel and Julian Rosenberg's appeals were denied, and the ghoulish moment of their executions was announced on radio and television. My mother, my brother, and I were up on Cape Cod on that date, beginning our family's summer vacation. My father had returned to Washington, D.C., to help in the struggle to gain clemency for the Rosenbergs. A number of organizations around the country worked at last-minute clemency attempts, though none ultimately succeeded. I recall listening to the radio broadcast that June 19 night at eight P.M. and hearing that these two parents (I was well aware that there were two young Rosenberg boys named Robert and Michael) had been executed. I also remember watching the tears roll down my mother's face as the news was reported, and feeling stunned that something like this could actually happen while, at the same time, my mother, Jeff, and I could sit on the patio overlooking Cape Cod Bay, serenely listening to the radio. The concept of "Duck and Cover" seemed pervasive in all walks of life. Bombs could drop from a blue sky and parents could be executed, spies could follow ordinary people and telephone lines could be tapped.

However, not everyone in the fifties was focused on issues of nuclear proliferation and the spread of communism. Housing was booming and developments were growing in city suburbs, roads were being built, and the Interstate Highway Act was signed in 1956, opening the country up to more mobility as motels became the new popular roadside inn. The AFL and the CIO merged, forming the country's largest federation of unions. Television commercials presented women happily doing housework, though in fact women were growing discontent about their rights in the workplace and in the bedroom.

Although newspapers and television journalists still rarely reported on issues relating to civil rights, that, too, was increasingly becoming a heated topic. On May 17, 1954, the Supreme Court unanimously decided in *Brown v. Board of Education* to legally end segregation. Disturbing racial incidents began showing up in the news that many people didn't want to hear about, like the story of a fourteen-year-old black boy named Emmett Till, who was beaten, killed, and thrown into the Tallahatchie River in 1955 by an angry mob of white men who believed Emmett had whistled at a white woman. In Montgomery, Alabama, on December 1, 1955, a black woman named Rosa Parks refused to give up her seat to a white man on a bus. She was arrested and charged with violating the segregation law of the Montgomery City code. The following day, the Women's Political Council officially endorsed a bus boycott, and three days later, on December 4, 1955, the Montgomery Bus Boycott was announced. The black community would not ride the buses in Montgomery, Alabama, for 381 days. Black churches were burned and Martin Luther King Jr.'s home was bombed on January 30, 1956, but the bus boycott was one of the most successful antisegregation movements that the country had yet witnessed. Moreover, besides sparking a movement against injustice, it also put the spotlight on the rising leadership of Martin Luther King Jr. But a year before Rosa Parks refused to give up her seat and a year before the Montgomery Bus Boycott—in the autumn of 1954, life was about to radically change for Jenniemae Harrington.

It had been a particularly cold autumn and the bite of winter was in the air. It was early October and the beginning of the short days and the long, dark nights. Jenniemae didn't much care for the cold or for the winter that would soon arrive, especially having been born in Alabama. Wintertime in Alabama was in no way similar to wintertime in Washington, D.C. Winter that year would be cold and damp. When the winds blew in off the Potomac River, the rain would turn into blinding sleet and the roads and sidewalks would become a slick sheet of black ice. A person couldn't walk more than two steps without risking a fall on the hard pavement. And if the sleet turned into a blizzard, then the buses would either run late—very late—or not at all. A person could wait outside at the bus stop for two, three, four, five, six hours before a bus would finally come creeping up the street. During sleet- or snowstorms, Washington was likely to be paralyzed. On days like this, with black ice on the sidewalks, Jenniemae, who lived just blocks behind the nation's Capitol in one of the city's poorest sections, walked very cautiously the five blocks to the corner bus stop, where she waited at a bus stop sign she couldn't read for the L4, the D.C. Transit bus that would take her "up" town. It was not uncommon for the jugglers—the drug dealers—to still be standing on the street corners or walking up and down the empty streets hoping to make one last deal before sunrise, hoping to make the last deal that would pay for their heroin or coke use from the night before or the night before that. Jenniemae knew most of them, the dealers and doers; they wouldn't bother her. She never carried more than penny cash and they knew it.

There was an unwritten word on the street that a man wouldn't mess with certain people if those people were trying to work an honest day's work. They especially wouldn't mess with a woman like Jenniemae, a good woman. This neighborhood was probably as safe a place as any for Jenniemae, even though it had the highest crime rate in the city. These dimly lit (if lit at all) streets were undoubtedly safer for Jenniemae than many of the white suburban streets outside downtown.

The bus wait was just one more wait in life, so as Jenniemae stood on the corner of Fourteenth and Nebraska one morning that fall, she was patient and uncomplaining. There would be no use in being otherwise. Impatience was one of those qualities reserved for the white man. They could allow themselves the luxury of being impatient because they expected better, and because life was supposed to treat them a certain way at a certain time. If things didn't move along accordingly, they had a right to be impatient and irritable. For a black person impatience had no purpose. It was as meaningless a consideration as wealth and riches, limousines and diamonds. So if the bus Jenniemae was waiting for was ten minutes late or four hours late, that was life and she would just stand there in the rain, snow, sleet, hail, sunshine, or fog, and wait.

Legal changes might have been under way within the buildings of the nation's capital, but these changes were certainly not visible on the streets. And even though D.C. might have been considered more forward thinking than many cities, it was not exactly a "liberal" northern city. The status of the black man in D.C. was what it was, and despite the inroads by people who tried to make things change faster, it benefited the white residents to make change go slowly or not at all. Life for most black people in D.C. was the same as it had been for the past hundred years. The Supreme Court had ruled in 1948, in *Hurd v. Hodge*, that restrictive housing covenants were unconstitutional, but the black people in D.C. still were living in a predominantly poor ghetto owned by white slumlords. In 1950, when eleven black children attempted to enroll at John Philip Sousa Junior High School in southeast D.C., they were asked politely to leave.

Which is why Jenniemae waited patiently. Once the bus arrived, she slowly climbed the narrow steps, retreated to the back, and found a seat. Once seated, she hoped that the warmth from the heaters positioned in the front would drift toward the back. Usually that didn't happen, and this morning was no different. Usually, with the opening and shutting of the doors at each stop, the heat didn't reach the back of the bus. The only warmth was from the bodies of the other black women and men. And though these insults were expected, it didn't mean that most of those sitting in the back of the bus didn't resent the insults. For a woman like Jenniemae, never one to complain, resentment boiled inside, particularly on cold mornings like this one. The only good thing she could have said about that day was that at least she was not alone—her people were sitting there alongside her.

By the time Jenniemae arrived at work, she had been awake for at least two and a half hours, having gotten up in her small, cold, run-down brick townhouse apartment that she shared with her sister, nieces, and nephews. She'd found her clothing in a dimly lit room, gotten herself something to eat in the tiny kitchen with its worn black-and-white linoleum flooring and an old metal stove with one working burner, and having ridden the three buses uptown to the groomed suburbs where she got off, she then proceeded to walk the mile to the alley behind our house, entering by the back door. Jenniemae's long route to work each morning took her from the slums of downtown D.C. to the back door of our white suburban house with black shutters and a wraparound porch.

On that morning the bus ride had taken longer than usual. By the time she reached work she already felt weary. It wasn't just the long ride and the cold morning; it was also that she had a bad feeling. It had begun the night before and lasted right on through to the morning. She had the bad feeling on the bus and kept wondering what it was and when it would show itself. It wasn't anything that she could put a finger on; it was just a sense of something about to go wrong—that something was off balance in her world. Jenniemae frequently sensed what might happen days ahead of time, and often those premonitions turned out to be true. She believed that there were signs—forecasts— of things to come or things that were meant to be and that a person had to pay attention to those signs in order to avoid possible catastrophes. "If the blind lead the blind, then both are gonna fall into the ditch," she always said, explaining why it was important for people to keep their eyes open to what was going on around them. Most people didn't pay attention, she said—they were blind—and if you followed them, you were going to follow them right into that same dirty ditch. She believed that only the Lord really knew for certain what was about to occur. She had a great disdain for weather forecasters and psychics. "Now, there are two blind men—the weather man and the psychic man. It's one thing to have the feeling 'bout what's comin' down the road, it's a whole other to say you know what it is," was how she phrased it. So when, on that cold morning, Jenniemae "had the feeling," it made her nervous from morning until nightfall. And when she left work that evening, that feeling hadn't gone away. She thought something bad was brewing . . . and she was right.

Jenniemae left work after washing the dinner dishes—around eight o'clock. She bundled up in her long black winter coat, tying a scarf around her neck and donning a wool cap. She again walked that mile to the bus stop for the L2 bus, which stopped at a corner on Connecticut Avenue, where she waited. That bus would take her a mile or so before she would have to transfer to a crosstown L6, and still later to the L4 bus, which would take her within blocks of her home. By the time she had boarded the L4, it was already close to nine-thirty. She wouldn't arrive home for another forty-five minutes at best. Only five other people—four black women and one black man—boarded the L4 with her that night. Over the course of the ride, people would get off or get on, mostly black people. Few white people rode the buses after dark, particularly traveling into southeast D.C.

Jenniemae was very tired. It had been a long day and that bad feeling had never left. What happened to Jenniemae in the hour or so that followed would change her life forever, and the entire incident might have gone unnoticed in our house for some time if Jenniemae hadn't completely unraveled a day later and James hadn't taken notice.

The next day, Jenniemae came to work more than two hours late. That in itself was out of the ordinary, since she was never that late. If she had chosen to make up a story about why she was late, life might have gone along as usual for a while. But it was not in Jenniemae's nature to lie. She wasn't the lying type. When she arrived at work late, she hadn't really considered what she was going to say. She was too upset, too distraught really, to offer an explanation for being a couple hours late.

As usual Jenniemae entered through the back door. It was close to eleven A.M., and the house was relatively quiet as she retreated to the back room. If someone had been at the back door when she arrived, they would have seen that her eyes were red and swollen from crying, but no one was there. Before beginning her work she sat down on the bed to gather her thoughts.

James was the only one home. When by eleven he hadn't heard the sound of Jenniemae climbing the stairs or a vacuum cleaner running, he grew curious. This seemed unusual. In fact, it occurred to him that he hadn't heard her telephone ring, which normally he could vaguely hear even from the back room, and he hadn't heard her usual soft humming or singing, something she did while dusting. Sensing that something was not right, he got up from his desk and went to look for her. Thinking she might be ironing or doing the wash, he first checked the basement but found it empty. He climbed the stairs and searched the rooms on the second floor, then the third and fourth floors. The only place he hadn't checked was the back room. It was not a place he felt particularly comfortable entering, since he considered it Jenniemae's private space. But now, having exhausted his search of the rest of the house, he had one more place to look. With great hesitation James passed through the kitchen and walked down the narrow hallway. The door to the room was slightly ajar, and as he approached, he thought he could hear sobbing. He stopped and stood very still, listening to the sobs. Finally he took the last few steps toward the half-opened door. He reached out and softly knocked twice. "Jenniemae?"

She responded with one word: "Yes?"

"Are you all right?"

She did not say anything.

"Jenniemae, are you all right in there?" he asked again.

Still she did not respond, but as he stood waiting he could hear her deep sighs, so he gently pushed the door open. She was sitting on the bed, her coat still on, bent over and crying.

"Jesus, Jenniemae, what is it?" he asked, genuinely concerned. She didn't look up.

"Jenniemae, what's wrong?"

She didn't look at him but said between sobs, "Ain't nothin'."

"It can't be nothing. It must be something."

"It's nothin'. Nothin'," she said, still sobbing.

"Jenniemae, it can't be nothing—tell me. Did something happen to somebody? Did something bad happen?"

But she couldn't speak.

"Jenniemae. What is it?"

"Nothin'."

"That is one bad nothing."

She did not respond.

"Please, tell me what it is. What happened?" he said. "Jenniemae . . . what is it?"

After a long sigh she said, "No, Mister James."

"What do you mean?"

"I can't say."

"Can't say what?"

"You can't know."

"Why?"

"It's not to know."

"Jenniemae. Please," he insisted, and after a long wait she finally replied.

"Mister James, you're not goin' to understand."

"Yes I will."

"No, Mister James. You can't."

"Please let me try. I'll just listen. Okay? Just listen," he pleaded.

And after a long pause Jenniemae finally said, "The busman."

"The busman?"

She just nodded her head.

"What do you mean, the busman?"

"It was the busman," Jenniemae responded.

"Who is the busman?"

"The busman that drives the L4."

"You mean the man that drives the bus you ride?"

Again she nodded.

"What? What did he do?"

"Oh Lord, Mister James," she cried.

"Jenniemae, please, just tell me what happened."

And after another long pause she said, "Last night. On my way home."

He waited, watching her.

Then she added, "He is hateful."

"Why?"

Jenniemae took her time before saying, "He has the evil inside . . . and is the evil."

"What did he do?"

"I can't, Mister James."

"Please tell me. I want to help."

"You can't."

"Just tell me, then," he pleaded.

After another long hesitation she continued. "That man is bad. Lord knows he's inside and outside bad. I have tried to turn away and not to pay attention to his words. I have told myself the man don't have a brain and don't know what he is sayin', but then he makes bad worse than evil, and—" She stopped.

"What? What in the hell did that busman do or say to you?"

"I can't say," she said, shaking her head as tears began streaming down her cheeks again.

"Can't tell? What do you mean? Tell me and maybe I can deal with this person."

"No, you can't be doin' that. Can't be," she said, sobbing again.

"There is no such thing as 'can't be.'"

"Yes there is."

"No," he insisted.

"You don't understand."

It took a moment before he responded to that. "Okay . . . okay, fine then . . . help me to understand here."

"I can't. I can't tell you."

"But why?"

"'Cause he said so." Jenniemae said softly.

"'He'? The busman?"

"Yes."

"What happened?"

"I can't tell if you are to go and be angry and do somethin', because that somethin' will make it worse for me."

"No it won't."

"Oh, yes it will."

"Okay," he agreed, "okay, just tell me and I'll promise not to do anything."

"That's a promise from you?"

"It's not just a promise from me, Jenniemae . . . it's a promise to you."

Jenniemae stared at the floor and was quiet for a long time before telling her story. "The busman started driving my route about a year ago . . . just about that long ago." She paused and tried to collect herself. "I remember when he came on to drive. We all pegged him right away. We all knew he had a badness to him. A person could tell. From the first day he had these dirty little white hands and small eyes that were circled with redness.

The dirt on those hands was always there—every single day—and it's a dirt that's in there so deep that it looks alive under his skin. We—all of us on the bus that first day—saw he was goin' to be a no-good man 'cause he had a hard look and a smart sass-talkin' way."

"How?" James was listening to every word.

"He thought he was so smart with all his niggers on the bus . . . like he owned us. Right off he goes and tells us, 'You niggers ain't more than nothin' to me, so don't be talkin' at me . . . and sit in the back like you supposed to do . . . and keep your mouths snapped shut so I don't hear your nigger talk.' And none of us were gonna talk back to him because he was the new man drivin' the bus and we all had to get where we were goin' to work." Jenniemae stopped, and stared hard at the floor again as if to steady her thoughts. "Then after a few months he tells us that we had to pay our money for the token transfer and we had to pay the extra to his pocket."

"Damn."

"So we had to do it . . . each of us payin' the extra money that he would put directly into his pocket. And then that extra money?" She paused. "Well, he would be sayin' that the extra was no longer extra enough, so it had to be more. The extra money was a bit more than the day before and a bit more than the day after that, and soon the extra money was most all any money that any of us had. And if you were a person who didn't have the extra money, you got yourself kicked off the bus. No matter if it was a rainy day or a snowin' day—it didn't matter to the busman. He would kick that person off and jus' go and laugh when he shut the door. It made my blood boil. But no one was gonna say nothin'. Especially not on the cold days when it was goin' on into the cold nights."

"And then what happened?"

"Then, oh Lord . . ."

"What happened?"

Jenniemae started to cry again.

"It's okay. Just take your time," he said, trying to calm her.

"Oh Lord. He . . . oh Lord, my . . . last night . . . the bus was going down Sixteenth Street and . . . it's a usual thing that I'm on that bus as the last one at night. And I always get off on the corner of Florida. But it was different last night . . . before he comes to Florida Street, he slows the bus up and I am thinkin' somethin' is not right. Somethin' is surely not right. And I have a bad feelin'. Real bad feelin'. And you know when a bad feelin' comes, it is there for a reason . . ." She stopped.

"What happened?"

"He . . . turns that big bus on to a street I don't know . . . that is nowhere . . . and he stops. Jus' stops. Then he goes and turns his light off. I am thinkin' to myself, *Oh, dear Lord, maybe there is somethin' wrong on the bus and . . .*"

"And what did he do, Jenniemae?"

She hesitated, took a deep breath, and started to sob. Between breaths she said, "He pushed on top of me and . . . did . . . you know. He did . . . you know he . . . did it to me and . . . then he laughed when I was cryin' . . . and when he was done he slapped my face and told me to get off his bus. He said that slap was nothin' to what he would go and do if I told anyone. He would enjoy killin' me, he said . . . no matter how big I was. And so I got off the bus in the dark night and I jus' started walking until I saw somethin' I knew and then I found the way to my home."

Jenniemae's sobs were long and deep. James was stunned. Angry and stunned. Neither of them said a word. He sat down next to her on the bed and placed one hand on her shoulder and rested it there, not quite certain what to do or say. Finally, after some time passed, he asked, "And then this morning . . . what happened this morning?"

Jenniemae said softly, "At first I thought maybe I wouldn't come on in here today . . . but then I am thinking I have to go sooner or later, and the sooner I get this done with is better. . . . It is sure better than to be thinkin' on it all day and makin' it worse and worser than it already is. So I made myself some hot water before I left my house. I told myself to pretend I was somewhere else and think about other things. I prayed to the Lord to help me and He tried His best. I know He did. I walked outside my house and down to the corner and waited at the bus stop. I kept thinkin' about breathin' and about the Lord being there for me. When that ugly bus came along, I began to think I was gonna stop breathin' because I couldn't catch my air. I thought I might die right then and there. Everything started to feel tight inside when the bus pulled up to the curb. I heard the Lord say to me, *Jus' pretend you're not here. Jus' pretend.* So I stared hard at the wheels, and when the wheels stopped going around and around, I knew it was time for the doors to open. And that is what happened. The doors opened and I said to myself, *It is time to put one foot in front of the other and keep goin',* which is what I did. I climbed on and got to that top step to put my money in and he says to me, 'Later.' But I didn't give him the satisfaction of lookin' him in the eye. I was too busy pretendin' I wasn't there."

"There won't be any later," James said emphatically.

"No, you can't be doin' nothin'. He'll kill me . . . and . . . you jus' can't."

Which was true and he knew it. Washington, D.C., might as well have been Hissop, Alabama, or Little Rock, Arkansas, or maybe anywhere else in the United States.

"You're never riding that bus again."

"I got to," she said.

"No, you don't have to."

"You're wrong. I have to, Mister James. I got to."

"No. You don't have to. It's over with that damn bus. I am driving you. I am picking you up every morning and driving you home every night."

"You can't be doin' that," she said.

"Oh, yes I can. I am going to drive you each way."

"You are not goin' to get yourself up and drive me in the mornings."

"Yes I will," he said proudly. "Yes I will."

They argued, but Jenniemae knew that he wasn't going to give in, and after that morning James became Jenniemae's private chauffeur. Every morning he picked her up in front of her home in the red Buick station wagon. He would arrive curbside just after the sun rose and in the evening he would give her a ride home. In the mornings she would be waiting in front of her house and in the evenings after he dropped her off he would watch her slowly climb the broken steps to her front door and would not pull away from the curb until she had opened the door, turned around, and waved good-bye. This routine continued for three months until one day Jenniemae demanded that it change.

"You are jus' not to pick me up in the mornings no more," she announced upon getting in the car one morning.

"Why is that?"

" 'Cause you can't and that is why."

"What do you mean, can't?"

"You are not pickin' me up in the morning, 'cause you look like a crazy man when you drive down here, and I don't want no crazy man pickin' me up no more."

"What?"

"Jus' that's what. People are talkin'. My people. They're sayin' I get picked up by a crazy white man every morning."

"Is that so?"

"It is so. You look all out of sorts in the morning. Like a crazy man."

"And?"

"Well, I can't be explainin' it to people down here that even though you are a crazy man, you're not a dangerous crazy man. And I can't be explainin' to them why I would be gettin' in the car with a crazy man. So you got to sleep and I got to find my way."

"No deal."

"We ain't talkin' about a deal here."

"But you can't take the bus. You can't. I won't let you."

"I appreciate it, Mister James. I really do. And you have a good heart to be drivin' down here, but I can do what I have to do."

"I really would rather . . ."

"I know what you're sayin' but, Mister James, this isn't the way."

"Well, maybe you're right. I do hate coming down here in the early morning. How about I agree I won't pick you up in the mornings but I'll still drive you home at night."

"Well, that's one good way."

"And one more thing," he added.

"What's that?"

"I would like it if you would agree to take a cab in the mornings."

"A cab?"

"Just in the mornings."

"No sir. That is costin' too much and I'd be lookin' like some rich lady down here. And then there would be the man climbin' through my window for money that I don't have," Jenniemae explained.

"Please. No bus. You just tell all those men to back off."

"Just tell them, huh? Mister James, I can't take a cab."

"Sure you can."

"Lord. I don't know."

"Jenniemae, please. Just do that for me. Please."

"Well, Lord . . . I suppose. I suppose."

"Then it's settled. I'll set it up."

"Mister James, I really appreciate this, but when things change I want to be ridin' the bus again. You understand me?"

"I do," James agreed, knowing that she meant that when that driver quit or was fired or was moved to another route, she wanted to just get on the bus like all her friends did and ride to work every morning.

The next morning, and for months thereafter, a Yellow Cab picked Jenniemae up and brought her to the house. In the evening James and Jenniemae drove the same route down Connecticut Avenue, turning onto K Street, then passing a few blocks north of the White House before heading past the Capitol and over to Second Street S.E., where he pulled up before Jenniemae's house. They talked about the weather, about the people walking the streets, or about the new buildings being constructed downtown. They discussed unimportant issues like new carpets for the house or the best onion soup Jenniemae ever made. When James pulled the car in front of Jenniemae's house, she would slowly maneuver her large body out of the car and say, "Thank you, Mister James. Good night now."

"Good night now, Miss Jenniemae."

# CHAPTER TEN

*"A one-eyed mule can't be handled on his blind side."*

In 1954, Senator Joseph McCarthy's obsession with communists, subversives, and spies in the United States peaked. Among the thousands on McCarthy's list of supposed enemies of the state was James, who was a mathematician, a Jew, a Roosevelt Democrat, a former SEC adviser, and a vocal opponent of the development of thermonuclear weapons. Obviously McCarthy knew all of this and suspected there might be more. If James was not any of what McCarthy thought him to be, it didn't matter; once he was on the list, he was assumed to be guilty.

Behind the fanfare of the McCarthy hearings the scientific community was increasingly wrestling with the conflict between the new physics of warfare—the hydrogen bomb—and the ethics or humanity of actually using such a weapon. The political community was also wrestling with the ethical implications of unleashing weapons of mass destruction, but given the heightened frenzy, they were equally anxious about who was and who was not to be trusted. McCarthy continued to feed the flames of fear and vociferously demanded that the subversive and dangerous individuals who were undermining the nation's safety be dealt with. Accusations of guilt were thrown about like confetti within the McCarthy circle. Once a person was accused of being a subversive, a communist, or a spy, his or her entire life was thrown into disarray. People lost their jobs, their friends, and their families, and some even resorted to suicide. A palpable sense of fear permeated the country. If you wanted to discuss something political, scientific, social, or economic, oftentimes it had to be done behind closed doors and in whispers.

In our house, my father did two seemingly contrary things: He put himself in the forefront of the heated political/scientific argument and then also closed the front doors in order to protect his family.

In a letter piece appearing in 1954 in *The Washington Post*, which was later collected along with many of his letters in *The Rule of Folly*, he wrote:

> ... if our generation is ever again to breathe easy—let alone survive—nothing will suffice short of an agreement which will mitigate the danger and fear of a sudden holocaust. We cannot escape the necessity of establishing a control system made effective by some form of inspection. The fundamental objective of a prudent plan must be an agreed level which would not permit the surprise unleashing of a major attack, not to say the waging of a major war. Proof that this level has been

established and is being maintained should be furnished by an inspection system directed to key points of national activity, which would inevitably reflect clandestine preparations for war.

We face the danger of a catastrophic war. The danger grows as the armories grow, as fear grows. We can neither avert war nor mitigate its effect by building ingenious engines. Only man makes wars and only man can prevent them. It is imperative that we reduce the tensions that lead to war.*

We went from a life in the light to a life in the dark. The heavy beige floor-to-ceiling drapes that hung over the living-room window—the same ones that were usually drawn back during the daytime—now were kept closed. The venetian blinds in the dining-room window also remained closed all day long. Overhead lights were left off until it was very dark outside, and only small reading lamps were turned on when needed. No one in our family asked why the inside of our house had undergone this transformation, but I recall thinking that something very dangerous must be going on outside.

My mother, who was working then on her doctorate degree in clinical psychology at the University of Maryland, came down with frequent migraine headaches. She fell into long bouts of depression and would disappear behind a closed bedroom

---

*James R. Newman, "Toward Atomic Agreement," in *The Rule of Folly* (New York: Simon & Schuster, 1962), p. 47.

door, or worse, at least for me, lie for hours motionless on the living-room couch with a damp cloth on her forehead. I assumed the migraines were brought on by the dangers outside, but as I would come to understand years later, they were undoubtedly caused by my mother's own personal demons. She was a woman of such low self-esteem that the thought of outsiders wanting to do her family or herself harm sent her into a state of intense paranoid depression. She took what was going on in the political arena personally, as though it resulted from something she, her husband, or even her children had done wrong. Ruth's thoughts might have been irrational but her depression was very real. Events outside of her control haunted her. Rather than choosing to fight or to confront a situation, more often than not she chose flight. She dealt with conflict by creating a screen of smoke both literally—chain smoking—and figuratively. She hid in her work and behind her art—writing, painting, sculpting, and doing needlework—often obsessively. She stayed up late many nights when involved with a painting or a sculpture. She became a quite talented, expressive, and interesting artist, going to art schools at night in D.C. during the winter months and taking classes throughout the day during the family's summer vacations in Truro, on Cape Cod. She made close friends with many artists, financially supporting more than a few when they were in need, and having relationships with more than one, both men and women. I believe her own exploration with art encouraged her to experiment with her emotions and her sexuality. There was one woman in particular who was a successful artist, had a terrific sense of humor, loved to tell stories, and was a proud nonconformist with whom my mother seemed to share a particularly close relationship. And given my mother's tendency to cross commonly accepted boundaries, it all seemed quite natural to me. I can't say that I ever worried about whether or not she had relationships with other women, or with men other than her husband. For her own part, my mother became a prolific artist, creating an impressive, if not sometimes unusual, body of oil and watercolor paintings, pastel drawings, clay sculptures, and enamel artwork. In fact, in some ways I believe her passion for art was one of the few things that helped to ground her when life was particularly complicated. However, when even art failed to bring her relief, she would become susceptible to painful migraine headaches.

As a child I struggled to understand my mother's sporadic withdrawal and depression and frequently blamed myself to some degree for her unhappiness, though I never quite understood exactly what it was I had done wrong or did not do right. I recognized, however, that even if I was partly the cause of her sadness, it was unlikely that I could change her moods. As I grew older I spent more and more time trying to understand the cause of my mother's emotional snares and entanglements while keeping my distance. While we were cautious with each other's feelings, more than once she attempted to explain herself. She described the intense loneliness she felt as an only child growing up and the abandonment she had experienced when her father left the family, choosing to travel from city to city, gambling, rather than spending time at home. And she related stories about the cruel nanny who routinely locked her in a closet when she misbehaved, causing her claustrophobia. She explained the deep sadness she felt as a young teenager upon losing her mother at the age of forty to breast cancer and then being forced to live with an uncle she disliked and distrusted. The uncle lived up to her intuitions by proceeding to embezzle whatever small inheritance my mother had been left, and then she made the difficult decision to leave the uncle's house and roamed from one friend's house to another until, at eighteen, she went to college on a scholarship. Her stories were vivid. They were filled with sorrow and hardships, and they were clearly filled with a sense of loss. If my mother were to describe herself, I believe she could have done it in one word: lonely.

My mother's distresses had a way of overtaking the house even when she wanted them to be hidden—probably most often when she wanted them hidden. Her fears were personal, they were social, they were economic, and they were also political. She feared that her husband might be taken away because of political circumstances, she feared that he might decide to leave her because of another woman, she feared that she might not succeed with her work, and she feared that her children would love her less or not love her enough.

The migraines usually began in early morning, lasted throughout the day and into the night. Some days were better than others, but when they were bad they were very, very bad, and on those days it was absolutely necessary that the house be quiet. And it soon became apparent—after weeks of these migraines—that even on a good day it was far better if the house remained quiet, just in case the headaches returned. Even James's current girlfriend, Sarah, who frequently spent the night in the small bedroom on the fourth floor, was kind enough to remove her spiked heels when she used the stairs.

Jenniemae approached this period of time with exaggerated optimism. Whether or not she actually felt optimistic, I'll never know. But she made an effort to arrive in the morning with a smile, a laugh, and a statement to the effect that this would be a new and glorious day.

If there was going to be darkness inside the house, then Jenniemae would find games for me to play in the dark, though mostly she encouraged me to play outdoors no matter how nasty the weather might be or how many men were sitting on stoops across the street or could be seen up the street watching our house from their unmarked cars. So I spent many of those dark-house days outside inhabiting our backyard oak tree, which had become my favorite hideout of all the ones I had by then created. The oak tree—at least in my memory—was the biggest on the block. It was taller than any other tree around and even taller than any nearby house. Its long, thick branches overlooked not only the back alley but also our neighbor's property. A massive trunk was covered by brown rippled bark and roots radiated out from the tree. Five feet above the base of the trunk the oak forked in four different directions, and each sturdy branch then forked in many other directions, which meant I could safely climb high branches in not just four ways but also eight or fourteen. For me, climbing that tree, finding the perfect spot each day, and watching everything that occurred in my bird's-eye view and everyone who passed underneath was more than just a way to pass the time. It was a way to escape.

One day Jenniemae suggested that I make a little house for myself in the crook of one of the stronger branches. I had never seen a house in a tree before.

"Honey, there are folks who live in treehouses—'cept in the lightning."

"Why not in the lightning?" I asked.

"Lightnin' is the fire," she told me, and then gave me a bit of advice I have always remembered.

"Beware of that big oak/It can draw in the stroke/Don't get near the ash/It will follow the flash."

So when it wasn't raining or threatening lightning, I lived in the oak tree, and with Jenniemae's guidance I constructed a very fine treehouse made of short wood planks, branches and twigs, rope, nails and twisted wire. That treehouse withstood all sorts of weather. As far as I know, it's still there today. From there I would watch the back alley of our neighborhood. I had a perfect spot to monitor the activities of the neighborhood birds, squirrels, deliverymen, and alley walkers. I would watch the garbageman, who twice weekly backed his green pickup down the alley to empty the trash containers, and I watched the knife-sharpening man, who came once a week in his old red truck, driving slowly down the alley, stopping at each house and calling out to see if anyone needed their knives sharpened. He knew I was there, though he pretended not to, which Jenniemae appreciated. I spent hours in that treehouse. Jenniemae would come out and check on me every so often and hand up cookies, cartons of milk, paper, and crayons. It was a fabulous house that made the darkness and tension seem less ominous.

Like me, Jenniemae disliked the heavy gloom that pervaded our home. When no one was looking she would open the curtains a little bit, and if no one noticed the crack of light shining onto the carpet, she would open the curtain a bit more. If neither of my parents discovered the open curtain by the afternoon, then wonderful long, thin shafts of sunlight would streak across the floor.

"It's not right to lock the sunshine out. A person needs light to live and children need it to grow right," she advised my father one afternoon when he had noticed that the curtains had been partially drawn open. "We have got to get the sun into this house, Mister James. I know you got your problems, and the Missus, she has them, too—and I know you call it complicated, but complicated is not a good way of life. A one-eyed mule can't be handled on his blind side. You have got to find a different way to lead that mule. Do you see what I am sayin' here?"

"No. Not really," he told her.

"The blind side is blind, Mister James. It can't see what it needs to see."

"I understand," he said, "but it's best to leave the curtains closed for now. One day it will change again. This storm will pass. Nothing remains the same for too long. It's a law of nature—storms pass."

"I do understand that, but how will you know the storm has passed if you're sittin' in the dark?"

# CHAPTER ELEVEN

*"Cuttin' the ears off a mule will not make him a horse."*

Sometimes you make a deal with God and it seems like that deal will be honored. Only later do you realize that there is no such thing as making deals with God. Whether that is because God doesn't take kindly to deal-making or the particular deal you tried to make wasn't good enough or there *is* no God is another problem. The end result is the same: Banking on deals with God is not a good idea.

Jenniemae's opinion on this matter was straightforward: "Deals don't work 'cause the Lord has His plate full enough and He can't go and make deals every single day 'cause there are too many people askin' for deals all the time. So, if'n He spent all His time makin' deals, then there wouldn't be no time left for the work He has to do."

This was as good a way as any to explain why some things turn out bad no matter how hard a person might pray. Jenniemae reminded us that the Lord could not be fooled by the looks of a thing. "The Lord knows. The Lord knows that what is goin' on in the insides of a man may not be the same thing that man is showin' on the outsides. He knows. The Lord, He knows. You can't be foolin' no Lord—no you can't."

Our house was a case in point. The way things looked on the outside did not at all reflect what was going on in the inside. The curtains may have been pulled for political reasons, but it wasn't only the light that was kept out of our house—it was also the truth. The curtains remained pulled for months, but even after they were opened again, the difference between the outside and the inside remained a secret. There was the outside truth and the inside truth, and some of those truths had to do with politics and some of them had to do with relationships, some had to do with economics and some had to do with intimacy, some had to do with numbers and mathematics and some had to do with love and fear.

"Do you think the Lord knows about our house?" I asked Jenniemae one day.

"Oh, He knows. Fo' sho' He knows. You can't be foolin' no Lord."

From the outside, our house looked tidy and inviting, but that did not accurately reflect what was transpiring on the inside. It seemed to me that life in our house was like one of those red apples that fell from our backyard apple tree. Those apples were about as shiny and glossy-looking as a red apple could possibly be. I always wondered if some God—maybe it was Jenniemae's God—had come down to the apple tree in the middle of the night or very early in the dewy morning and put a shine on all those apples, because the apples on other trees never looked as shiny as the ones on our backyard tree. Those apples were so shiny that I always wanted to pick them off the ground and just bite into them. Jenniemae warned that we all had to wash those apples before eating them because "Lord knows, you can't be eatin' fallen apples like that. The outsides don't always tell the story. They be lookin' one way and they be really another way. You take a bite and Lord knows what will happen to you."

"How about if I reach up and pluck the apple straight off the tree?" I asked Jenniemae.

"Nope. Insides and outsides, insides and outsides. Two different things."

Which meant that we were not allowed to eat the shiny apples, whether plucked from the branches or picked from the ground, without Jenniemae's inspection and a thorough washing with soap and water. Unfortunately, I didn't apply the lesson about the difference between the outsides and the insides of a thing to other arenas of life in the house, which was why I had no idea what was transpiring as Jenniemae's stomach grew larger and larger each week. Because Jenniemae was already very overweight, an extra five or ten pounds—while it might be noticeable in most people's bodies—wasn't with her. And if I did notice it, I would never have assumed anything more than that she was eating more and therefore gaining weight. However, James watched the weight gain and worried. Week by week he watched as Jenniemae's belly grew larger. Sometimes he wondered what she might be thinking but he never asked. Sometimes he hoped that what he thought might be going on wasn't.

However, wishing a thing so rarely made it the case. As the months went by, Jenniemae's body changed more and more; she grew rounder, her breasts enlarged, her cheeks flushed when she climbed the stairs, and she became short of breath while making up a bed. James could no longer deny what was happening, and his suspicions turned from the possibility of a thing to the likelihood. He realized that she would not want to bring the matter up and, truth be told, he didn't really want to bring it up, either. With each passing day James watched Jenniemae struggle as she moved around the house to get her work done.

One afternoon, about four months after Jenniemae was raped, I joined my father on one of his ritual daily walks. Sometimes it took a bit of convincing on my father's part to get me to join him—it wasn't that I didn't enjoy walking with him, it was more that the idea of walking seven miles (which was his usual distance) was not something a ten-year-old particularly would choose to do. Then there was the additional fear factor that accompanied these walks. It was not uncommon for my father to experience severe chest pains when we walked, and when this would occur, he would slow his pace or stop walking entirely and place his index and middle fingers on his wrist or against the side of his neck in order to check his pulse. Sometimes we would stop for a fairly long time while he sat on a curb or an empty bench to rest. When he felt up to it, we would resume walking and inevitably he would rest his right hand over his heart as we strolled down Connecticut Avenue, Wisconsin Avenue, Massachusetts Avenue, or through Rock Creek Park. Though we never discussed what was happening—there was no mention of a possible heart attack even though he had had five previous heart attacks over the years—there was also no question that I was well aware that my father's health was precarious. I silently worried about that all the time—at night, during the day, and on these walks. However, no matter how uncomfortable those walks might turn out to be, I rarely wanted to disappoint my father, and when asked, I almost always joined him.

On this particular afternoon he asked, "Do you think Jenniemae is pregnant?" To a child back then the idea that someone who wasn't married could be pregnant was out of the question, and the possibility that Jenniemae in particular could be pregnant was beyond comprehension. Jenniemae was the one stable person in our house and in my life. I could depend on her for advice, for being where she said she was going to be each day, for acting the same, for not having long bouts of dark depression, for not disappearing for many days with various women, for being understanding, attentive, motherly, and soft spoken. Being pregnant did not fit anywhere into my idea of Jenniemae, not to merttion that I loved Jenniemae like a parent, and if she was pregnant and had a child, then where would I fit in?

"What? What do you mean?"

"I think she might be pregnant. Haven't you noticed her belly growing?"

"But . . ."

"I think she is," he said, looking drawn.

"That's not possible. How could she be pregnant?" I asked, but he wasn't about to answer that question.

"It is possible. And I think she is. Someone has to talk with her about it. She's all alone."

"Alone? What do you mean, alone? She has her sister and she

has us," I suggested, not picking up on the point that pregnant women usually had men in their lives who cared for them.

"She does have us, doesn't she," he said.

"Isn't John-John there to take care of her?" I assumed he was the father of any possible child.

"Not for this," my father simply said.

"Why not?"

"He just can't be. Not this time."

The following morning, when Jenniemae brought James his tea, she looked tired and troubled as she set the cup and saucer on the desk. He paused from his work, put down his pen and eyeglasses, and looked up at her. Her eyes were red and swollen.

"Jenniemae?"

Tears ran down her cheeks.

"Jenniemae, please sit down here for a minute. Let's talk."

Jenniemae shook her head.

"Please. Let's just talk a minute."

"No, Mister James. Not now."

"I think I know what's going on here," he said.

"Oh Lord, Mister James, you can't know."

"But I do. And we can deal with this . . . well, because we have to deal with it . . . and because there is a tomorrow."

"Not always," Jenniemae said very softly. "Ain't always a tomorrow."

"We might not be around for all the tomorrows, but there still is one. Even if there is no us and even if there is no earth, there is always such a thing as tomorrow." He began to go off on a theoretical tangent but pulled himself back. "Okay, okay, forget that now. Let's talk about this. This is serious and I need to know what you want to do?"

"What do you mean?"

"What do you mean, what do I mean? I'm talking about what to do here."

"There ain't nothin' but nothin' to do," she said.

"Wait a minute; there is more than nothing. There are some choices. You could choose to not keep this . . . you know . . . if you don't want to . . . which I assume you probably don't. There are lots of families who would love to have a baby," he said, embarrassed to be talking to her in this way.

"No, no, no. Lord, Lord no, Lord no," she said, understanding perfectly well where he was heading. "No choices like that."

"But it is possible . . ."

"No sir, there is no turnin' this around in any sort of way. It is what it is and it is what is happenin', because that is the Lord's way no matter if I understand it or you understand or neither one of us understands it. And it is best not to be discussin' a why about it. No sir. Lord knows, there are some things worthy to talk about and then there are some other things not worthy to talk about, and this, Lord knows, this is one of those things."

"No, that's not true. It may be just one of those things, but a person can do something about it."

"I can't be discussin' what I can't listen to."

"Have you been to a doctor?" he asked, and then answered himself: "No, I know you haven't."

"Ain't goin' to one, either."

"Why?"

" 'Cause. Not goin' to be doin' that."

"And the baby will be born how? Who will be there?" This was the first time there was even the mention of a baby.

"What do you mean?"

"What do you mean, what do I mean?" he asked, confused.

"Okay, Mister James, you got to slow down here. This is one thing that is my problem and not yours to own."

"True, but it is my problem."

"No it ain't. It ain't you that this is happenin' to, and it ain't you that is to be dealin' here."

"I know that but you're wrong," he replied.

Jenniemae stared at him before saying, "Wrong? This is not happenin' to you."

"It is, though. Sure, I'm not the one who was harmed and directly affected, but . . . well . . . but it is happening to me because I care about you," he said, embarrassed.

The room became silent and Jenniemae shifted her weight from one leg to another before saying quietly, "Which I do thank you for, Mister James, but you need to understand somethin'. Listen to me. And listen to me good. You folks do things in a different way than my folks do. My people . . . when a thing happens to my people, it is jus' another thing that happens. That's jus' all there is to that. We look at a thing straight in the eye—no matter if it is evil or good—and we head right on into livin' with it. For us, there isn't such a thing as changin' a thing jus' 'cause it happened. There is jus' livin' with it. Now, for you

folks it is a different matter. It is not the same. With you folks
when something bad happens you jus' figure you can up and
change it. You almost know you can up and change it. So when a
bad thing happens to you folks, you just say, Well, sure, now I
will change that to be better. And sometimes that changin' is for
the better and then some other times the changin' of a thing is
not for the better at all." Jenniemae stopped for a moment to
make sure he was listening, which he was. "So there are things
and there are things. Now, this thing that happened to me has
happened to me, and I do 'preciate your tryin' to help here, but I
have to do this my way and not your way."

"I understand, but maybe you could just do one thing differently. Like see a doctor," he began, but she interrupted.

"Now, do you think that there would be any of my people
standin' here on this planet if we had to wait for doctors to be
helpin' us along? No, I don' think so. There wouldn't be none of
us here at all if we had to be waitin' on your doctor folks to help
us along. No sir. So I 'preciate that, too, but it ain't happenin',"
she said.

"But sometimes a doctor is necessary. Sometimes babies get
born and they're in trouble. Well, I mean they need help and the
mother . . . well, she needs help. I'll help you get a doctor and I'll
pay for it. It can still be secret. And then you could just consider
giving it up for adoption right after—"

"No. No matter how it came to be, this is still the Lord's
child, and no matter that the devil entered into my life, there is
a reason for that and it is only the Lord's reason to know. So if

the Lord knows—which He does—then He is watchin' over me and this little one. I am not goin' to think about this one minute more. You hear me?"

He knew that every option he might suggest and every conceivable ounce of reason he might put forward was useless. Whatever was going to happen was going to be directed by Jenniemae, and he would just have to sit back and support her as best he could. Jenniemae was not about to let him direct her in any way on this issue.

# CHAPTER TWELVE

*"Better the gravy than no grease at all."*

As the months passed and Jenniemae's belly grew larger, James became ever more solicitous about her health. Although my father knew, and I now also was aware that Jenniemae was going to have a baby, it was not openly discussed. My mother may have known or suspected that Jenniemae was pregnant but, as far as I knew, she never brought it up. And Jeffrey, too, may have noticed, but this was not something he and I would have discussed. So the weight gain—noticed or not—went unmentioned. When Jenniemae was six months pregnant, James told Ruth that he wanted her to hire one more maid for the house. Never once was Jenniemae's condition mentioned; he simply suggested that cleaning this large a house required more than one person.

"We need one more maid here," he said.

"Why? Isn't Jenniemae enough?" she asked.

"No, she isn't. The house is large and we need one more. It's too much for one person."

"That's ridiculous," she insisted.

"It's not."

"It wouldn't be too much if she lost some weight and could get around better."

"It has nothing to do with her weight. Jenniemae gets around as quickly as anyone. It's just too much work for one person to do every day. I want one more maid hired. Let's not argue about it and just do it."

"You would think Jenniemae was your new girlfriend the way you take care of her."

"She is a good, hardworking woman who is being asked to do too much. All I am asking is that you hire another maid. If you can't see to that, then I'll make some calls myself."

"Fine, fine. I'll call the service tomorrow."

And the following week a new maid, Serena, was hired to help out. Although Jenniemae resented having anyone else in "her house"—and she did consider it her house—she was silently thankful to have someone else climb the four flights of stairs every day.

The morning Serena arrived, I saw a side of Jenniemae that none of us had ever seen before. Rather than the generous, kind, helpful woman we knew, Jenniemae transformed into a tyrant. Serena was no more than seventeen years old, with black hair neatly tied back in a bun in order to make her look older, about five feet tall, underweight, and extremely shy. Jenniemae took every advantage of that shyness, barking orders at her, even hissing through her teeth while correcting her when she felt something was done improperly.

James seemed to enjoy Jenniemae's dictatorial style, though it was difficult not to feel sorry for Serena. "Tell her to clean the top two levels, Jenniemae," he suggested, purposely never mentioning her name. "Her" became Serena's name around the house. "Her," which was a pronoun we were distinctly prohibited to use when addressing or talking about any person we knew. It was impolite, we were always told, to say "her," "she," "he," or "him" when speaking about someone in their presence. But Serena was referred to as "her" or "she" by both James and Jenniemae. Demeaning Serena became a blood sport.

"You know, she's not gonna do any kind of good job up there," Jenniemae insisted. "You know that. She doesn't know this from that and that from this. Child must have grown up in the dirt swamps."

"I don't really care how good a job it is and where she grew up, just so she does it decently," James said.

"That's fine by you but not fine by me. And another thing—I got to make sure that when she's done in the afternoon she gets on out of here so she doesn't steal somethin' from the house or get under my feet while I'm busy cookin' the dinner. I don't need some woman botherin' me when I'm cookin', and you don't need a robber in your own house."

"True enough. You keep an eye on her, and whatever you tell her is just fine, but make sure she takes up her own load of work now. You're the boss, okay?"

"Oh, I will make sure of it, and I'm as mean a boss as they come. But better to be mean up front than swept clean in the end, Mister James. Better mean than swept clean."

# CHAPTER THIRTEEN

*"The crow and the corn can't grow in the same field."*

As the weeks passed Serena came out of her shell and started to rebel against the constant harassment and barked orders from Jenniemae. The two of them began to argue. Serena refused to re-clean rooms that she'd already cleaned. Serena didn't want to polish the silverware every other day. Serena didn't want to hang all the shirts Jenniemae ironed. "You hang 'em yourself after you iron 'em," Serena told her. "You're right there with 'em, so why can't you hang 'em up?" The more she argued a point, the more Jenniemae insisted that it be done. But most of all Serena didn't like being suspected of thievery or called names. "You can't be trusted," Jenniemae would say. "Not one bit. Just look at the way you hang your head—just the way a weasel hangs his head. Can't be trusted. Weasel. Hawk. Vulture." One afternoon while the two were arguing Jenniemae almost fired her.

"Didn't your mama ever teach you to clean properly under a thing? Not just the top sides, but the bottom sides, too? Are you a blind weasel or what? Seems like you got no mama to show you right from wrong," Jenniemae yelled at her.

"I'm not blind and I got myself a fine mama and I'm not listenin' to you talkin' bad about her. Not one bit, not for one minute. I cleaned under and sideways on that thing there," Serena said, trying to hold her own.

"No sir, you didn't clean down there. And don't tell me you did a thing you didn't do. One thing I can't take is a lyin', stealin' weasel woman."

"I don't lie. I don't steal and you're not the hirin' lady here, so who are you to tell me? I'm not 'bout to listen to your yellin' and such."

"You best be listenin' to me. I may not have hired you—and Lord only knows if you should have been hired, anyways—but I surely can be the one to fire you," Jenniemae hissed.

Serena just shook her head in disgust and walked off.

"You best to be listenin' to what I say," Jenniemae yelled at her.

It was during that argument that finally James did intervene and suggested that Jenniemae not push Serena too hard or the young girl might up and quit, and it would be hell to pay if he had to ask Ruth to hire another maid.

"Maybe you should lighten up a bit on her," he suggested.

"The crow and the corn can't grow in the same field, Mister James."

"I know, but you need her now, too."

"Maybe."

"And here I thought I was difficult? You need to focus on the weeks and months you have left before this little one is born. You need a calendar."

"A what?"

"A calendar to show you the days."

"I know the days. I don't need no calendar."

"Sure you do. It's a great tool."

"Tool? I don't need a tool. I got more than plenty of tools. Tools to clean. Tools to iron. Tools to cook. What I have a need for is some peace around here."

"Just listen a minute," he said, trying to take her mind off the new cleaning girl.

"I don't need a calendar to take care of this girl not doing her job."

"No, but a calendar would help to see how many days you have before she leaves this house."

"Well . . ." Jenniemae paused.

"Just give me one minute. Calendars are good things to use. They have a great history . . . and it has to do with the moon," he told her.

"Is that so? The moon?"

"Absolutely the moon. The first calendars were made thousands of years ago and they were based on the lunar phases— the different moon phases, like whether it was a full moon or a half moon or a sliver."

"I know moon phases. You don't have to be explain' all of that."

"Sorry. I didn't mean to insult you. I just wanted to explain my story."

"I'm okay with that," she agreed. "Go on then."

"Well, a long time ago some wise Egyptian men came up with a way to separate each day and night from the next day and night. Their idea was based on the seasons and the phases of the moon, and it seemed like a clever way to record events. When they first drew up their idea, called a calendar, they had three seasons and each one had four months. There was the Flood time, the Seed time, and the Harvest time."

Jenniemae listened carefully. "You can go on," she said, and he smiled.

"Okay, then. Then the Babylonians came along and they made their own calendar but did it differently. They had twelve lunar months—moon months—and each month began after a new moon. Then along came the Greeks, who came up with their version, which was similar but not exactly the same. Two thousand years ago there were about a hundred different calendars being used by different societies."

"Is that right?"

"There was the Muslim calendar and the Hebrew calendar, the Aztec and Mayan calendars—different calendars, but they had in common one idea." He paused and Jenniemae quickly added, "The moon. That was the one idea, right?"

"Right." James was pleased.

"Lord have mercy, that was one good notion, because the moon is heaven's light at night."

"And it is a good guide to count the days gone by and the days to come in the future. It is a great way to plan, so you might like to have a calendar to watch the days before this event is due to happen."

"Maybe."

"You could have this calendar on my desk. I have another in the closet."

"Where do I begin it?" Jenniemae asked after James handed it over to her. "Where is the today box?" James showed her where the present date was located and how to mark the next date and all the days after that. Jenniemae took the calendar and kept it in her room. Each day she marked off a square by filling it in with black ink, leaving a corner of the box available for drawing the size of the current moon. When there was a full moon, she drew a circle, and as the moon waxed or waned, she drew that shape. Without the words of the days of the week or the names of the months printed anywhere, Jenniemae knew which box represented a Monday, which a Tuesday, a Wednesday, Thursday, Friday, Saturday, and Sunday. She understood that a month was over when all the boxes had been filled in and a new month began with a new piece of paper full of empty boxes.

One day James advised, "Mark the days on the calendar but don't wish them away. Take care of every minute; otherwise hours slip away and days are lost."

"That's the truth, Mister James, sure is," she agreed. "I look forward to a thing so bad that I can't for the life of me remember what I need to know about today."

"Happens to me all the time. There was a man who once said, 'Half our life is spent trying to find something to do with the time we have rushed through life trying to save.'"

"Lord have mercy, that's the truth isn't it?"

# CHAPTER FOURTEEN

*"Beginning is the start of what will come to be."*

On May 29, 1955, Jenniemae Harrington gave birth to a baby girl at her home in southeast Washington, D.C. Her sister and niece were by her side. The baby was born about a month prematurely. This birth was not announced in *The Washington Star* or *The Washington Times*; however, Jenniemae was as proud as any mother could be and named her beautiful baby girl Lilac Belle Harrington.

Though Lilac Belle was her given name, she would always be called Lila Belle or just Lila. Jenniemae chose Lilac because that was her favorite flower. Lilacs, she said, had the most beautiful delicate purple and pink petals, and they smelled sweeter than heaven and blossomed with glory, just like this baby girl. She added the name Belle because that was Ruth's mother's name. Although Jenniemae had never met Belle, she explained that Ruth's face became softer whenever she mentioned her deceased mother's name. Jenniemae believed that if Belle were still alive, Ruth would be a more patient and gentler woman. Jenniemae didn't know much about Missus Ruth's past, but she had been told that Ruth's father had left the family when she was very young and her mother had died a few years after that. In Jenniemae's mind mothers were more crucial than fathers for bringing a child up, and it was clear to her that the loss of Missus Ruth's mother had created a dark hole in her heart.

Ruth wasn't always the easiest woman to work for, but Jenniemae believed she understood her, and no matter the impatient quips, particularly in the morning, Jenniemae really did like her. She admired Missus Ruth's independence and her work ethic, though Jenniemae was aware that Ruth often looked tired, tense, and overworked. It also was obvious that Missus Ruth had a sadness about her, and that particular look, whether understandable or blurred, on a white face or a black one, was not foreign to Jenniemae. Sadness didn't discriminate. While Jenniemae wasn't privy to Ruth's inner secrets, she was aware that Mister James's women—the ones who came and went, came and went, came and went and sometimes even lived under the same roof—tore Missus Ruth's spirit down, even though it wasn't discussed. Jenniemae quietly watched as Missus Ruth pretended that what was obviously painful did not hurt. And Jenniemae (though she never would have articulated it) probably suspected that should Missus Ruth show any emotion, any pain, any anger about the girlfriends, Mister James might abandon her. With every new woman who appeared as James's lover, there was a new hurt, and all these hurts were like bricks being laid one on top of the other, creating an invisible wall between Missus Ruth and her family. So every time that Missus Ruth appeared short-tempered and impatient, Jenniemae tried to look beyond it. Unlike the way in which she behaved with James, giving back much of what he dished out, Jenniemae treated Ruth with a seriousness that seemed appropriate. There was not the edginess or humor that Jenniemae had developed with Mr. James, but nevertheless she liked Ruth very much.

So Lilac Belle Harrington was the name she chose.

# CHAPTER FIFTEEN

*"Ain't no use askin' a cow to pour you a glass of milk."*

Lila Belle was born at home on a Sunday, for which Jenniemae was grateful because it was the day of the Lord. And even though the baby was born a few weeks earlier than expected, it was good luck to be born on a Sunday. It was the Lord's way of telling Jenniemae that everything would be just fine and that the child would be forever under His watchful eye. "He is watchin' no more and no less than every other thing He is watchin'. He is watchin' every sparrow that falls from the sky and every baby born on earth, but He is especially keepin' an eye out for those children born on a Sunday. That is a good-luck sign, sure 'nough, but there wasn't one dog that could be heard howlin' in the dark part of the night, which is 'nother good-luck thing."

The other added blessing was that Jenniemae would not miss a day of work. "Talkin' about a fire doesn't boil the pot," she allowed, explaining why it was important to work every day.

The next day, Jenniemae arrived at work on time at seven A.M., appearing tired but happy. Walking up the path that led to the back side of the house, she was surprised to see my father at the door waiting to greet her. He didn't know that she had just given birth twenty-four hours earlier though he knew the baby would arrive sometime soon. In fact, a few days before she gave birth, Jenniemae had said in passing, "This one will be arrivin' on a Sunday."

"How do you know?"

"I jus' know."

"Do you want to make a wager on this?"

"Oh no, Lord ha' be no. I jus' know when there is a right time and a right place for this baby to come into the world. And this one, she knows to be born on a Sunday."

"She? How do you know the baby is a girl?"

"I jus' know. I jus' know."

And, of course, Jenniemae was right—it was a Sunday and it was a baby girl. And when she came to work the following morning, Jenniemae looked relieved though weary. And when he asked, "And?"

She responded, "She's here."

"Well, congratulations! That's wonderful. But why did you come in today? You should have stayed home."

"I have to come to work."

"Where is she?"

"She is with my sister and bein' cared for jus' fine."

"What's her name?" he asked. He wondered what she looked like but didn't want to ask. Was she more white than brown or more brown than white? Did she look like the bus driver or did she look like Jenniemae?

"Lilac Belle . . . and I know what you're wonderin' on, Mister James."

"What do you mean?"

"I know what you're thinkin' because I thought 'bout it, too. My Lila—she is jus' lookin' like coffee with cream, which is okay by me. Don't think that I wasn't worried on it. Because I was. I fretted on it—thinkin' that she might look . . . well, you know, more the likes of your people than her own. And the Lord knows we don' need white babies in the ghetto," she said, half laughing. "It's hard 'nough bein' black in the ghetto, much less you go and find yourself with a white baby in a black mama's arms. Lord no! No," she insisted. "But I gave her that entire name so as to give her every sort of dignification in the world."

Stunned with her capacity to so easily read his mind—God knows, he thought, his own wife couldn't do that—he was speechless. "Lilac Belle?"

"Yes, isn't that pretty?"

"Truly, it is. And the Belle? Is that from . . . ?"

"Yes it is. Missus Ruth says that her mama, Belle, had as good a heart as any woman she ever knew."

"I'm sure she did." James had never met his wife's mother, though he had some doubts about how Belle from Shreveport, Louisiana, would have liked her name being given to a light brown baby.

It was a pretty name. And Ruth was clearly surprised when told by her husband that Jenniemae had had a baby. The extra pounds on Jenniemae's already large frame hadn't been very noticeable, and even if she had suspected anything unusual was transpiring, Ruth would never have asked Jenniemae about her weight gain. However, Ruth was definitely shocked when she heard that the baby's middle name had been given in honor of her own mother. She thought it was a nice gesture on Jenniemae's part though she wasn't quite certain how to respond to it. It bothered her to think that Jenniemae had reached out in this way even though Ruth had never done much to reach out to Jenniemae. Sometimes, Ruth considered, the people you least suspect to be a part of your life are a part of it, anyway. She hadn't exactly pushed Jenniemae away—but then she had never been open for much of any relationship with her, either. Naming the baby Lilac Belle not only surprised Ruth but made her feel a bit guilty for not taking the time to be personable and not having the patience with Jenniemae. She felt that she should try to do better. She would buy the baby a gift. And the next day she did just that. Ruth bought Lilac Belle a pink blanket with purple flowers embroidered on the borders.

"Lilacs," she told Jenniemae.

"Yes indeed. Those are some beautiful lilacs all around this pretty blanket. Thank you very much, Missus Ruth. My baby be sleepin' with pretty flowers."

"I wish you all the best. Maybe one day I will meet her."

"I 'ppreciate that. One day soon, Missus Ruth. One day soon. And thanks to you again."

"Thank you, Jenniemae. I like her name."

"I do, too, Missus Ruth. I do, too."

# CHAPTER SIXTEEN

*"Death don't see no difference*

*'tween the big house and the cabin."*

Lila Belle's arrival was one of the very few bright spots for the entire family after a long, hard winter and a bleak, damp spring. From January through April there had been one gray day after another. It snowed. It drizzled. It rained. And the cold winds that usually waned by March's end had continued through April and into May. When daylight savings time arrived, Washingtonians found that instead of gaining an extra hour of warmth and sunshine, they faced another hour of visible drizzle. Even the cherry blossoms bloomed later than usual.

During this gray spring James reported one evening at dinner that when he walked the path through Rock Creek Park and passed the lower entrance to the National Zoo, he had noticed that the duck pond, which was usually crowded and noisy with baby mallards by now, had not one duck in it. This was very unusual. He also said that there was a peculiar chill in the air that seemed to him to forecast a chill besieging the planet. From the way he described his afternoon walk, it was clear to all of us around the table that the chill had more to do with him than it had to do with the planet.

Darkness and death seemed to be on his mind more than usual—and death was no stranger even on the best of days. He had been thinking about dying since he was a small child. It was such a constant companion that in some ways he became used to it, the way you become used to looking both ways before crossing a street. But now it wasn't simply his own mortality that bothered him, it was everyone's: friends and relatives, acquaintances and absolute strangers, humans and animals, trees and plants.

Totally apart from the dismal weather, it had already been a difficult year. In January a group of scientists at Columbia University had developed an atomic clock that maintained accuracy within one second per three hundred years. Though one might have assumed James would have found this exciting, he didn't. He didn't like the idea of time being measured with accuracy, because time was an illusion, anyway. In March, Alexander Fleming, the British biologist who discovered penicillin and with whom James had become friends in London, died. The jazz great Charlie Parker also died in March; he never knew Charlie Parker but liked his bebop sound. And then on April 18, Albert Einstein died. That hit James very hard. They had been friends and colleagues, particularly in their mutual fight against the proliferation of thermonuclear weapons. They had laughed together and shared political sympathies. They frequently spoke on the telephone, and there were the spring visits to Princeton that James had always looked forward to.

Every year in June, our family left the heat and humidity of

D.C. to spend three months at our summer home on Cape Cod. We traveled in two separate cars—oftentimes my father and I in one car and my brother and mother in another—and we went our separate ways at separate times. If schedules permitted, my father and I would stop at Dr. Einstein's house in Princeton on the first leg of our long drive. Before the New Jersey Turnpike was completed in 1952, that drive from D.C. to Princeton would take up to twelve hours. My father always insisted on leaving no later than four A.M. in order to avoid the Baltimore traffic and clear Wilmington, Delaware, by nine. Once in New Jersey, we would continue north along U.S. 130 until we hit U.S. 1. It was a long, slow drive on two-lane roads that were poorly maintained, and we would hope for a cool day, since there was no such thing then as air-conditioning in cars. Our car was packed with books, legal pads, a typewriter, documents my father was working on, suitcases, and our two large dogs, both English setters. The dogs were brother and sister; Molière, the female, had black spots and Mozart, the male, had liver brown spots. Like brothers and sisters, Molière and Mozart frequently fought for the one open window in the back—the other window could not be rolled down because of the many boxes stacked against it— and my father reprimanded them as if they were squabbling children. Once, in fact, Mozart came very close to pushing his sister out the back window. Had it not been for my father grabbing Molière's tail with one hand while driving with the other, Molière would never have completed that trip.

The goal was always to reach Princeton in the afternoon in order to give my father and Dr. Einstein ample visiting time.

Even though these visits were scheduled in advance, my father liked to stop at a gas station miles before we reached Princeton and telephone to say that he was almost there. Once we arrived at Dr. Einstein's unassuming house on Mercer Street, my father would park our station wagon, then, leaving the dogs inside the car, he and I would walk to the front door, ring the bell, and wait for the maid to answer. Although she knew we were expected, she would inevitably ask my father why he was there, what he wanted, and whether or not he had given Dr. Einstein advance notice. Only moments later Dr. Einstein would appear wearing his usual wool sweater, no matter the temperature outside, and reprimand her for being rude, particularly to me.

"Just a little girl. Just a little girl!" he would say, and then ask us where the dogs were. When told they were in the car, he would lead us back to the station wagon. Dr. Einstein, an animal lover who had had a dog named Chico, would delight over our dogs and insist that we let them out and that we all go for a walk together. He enjoyed taking us along a wooded path that led to a creek. Beside the creek, under a favorite maple tree, there was a wooden bench where Dr. Einstein and my father would sit and talk while I played with the dogs. Usually my reward for not disturbing them was that later I would be treated to a vanilla ice cream cone, which Dr. Einstein said was the best flavor to enjoy on a hot day. He believed that dogs enjoyed that flavor equally well and always treated them to the final licks of the cone. Those were the times that James would not easily forget, nor could he replace them. Thinking about Dr. Einstein's death depressed him terribly, even though the wonderful physicist was

James at his desk
*Photo by Philippe Halsman © Halsman Archive*

seventy-six and hadn't been expected to live much longer since he had previously suffered an abdominal aortic aneurysm.

A week after Dr. Einstein passed away, another good friend of James's—a chess companion—suffered a heart attack and died only hours after the two had played chess together. James mentally replayed their chess game over and over again, as if changing the course of that particular game might change the death of his friend. Death and dying seemed to be everywhere. As one death followed another, James began to add them to some invisible list. There was the ninety-eight-year-old grandmother of a colleague—a woman he had never met—who died from old age. James took to thoroughly reading the newspaper obituaries right after scanning the headlines. One afternoon he read that a neighbor down the street, Mr. Rigley, whom he had never met, had recently died of a heart attack, leaving a wife and two children behind. A World War II pilot named Charles Ralston, who lived six blocks away—another stranger—died in his sleep. A ten-year-old girl named Sheila Mitchelle was killed when hit by a car while riding her bicycle down Thirty-fourth Street. A forty-six-year-old newspaper reporter for *The Washington Post* was killed in an airplane crash. A fifty-one-year-old insurance agent with three children and a wife who worked for Prudential died. And then there was the squirrel he'd seen just the other day: He had watched it get run over by a delivery truck. The squirrel looked so innocent running across the street, having scurried down one tree on the north side in order to dash up another on the south side, and the delivery truck flattened it without the driver ever hitting the brakes. James didn't miss the squirrel or Mr. Rigley or Charles Ralston or Sheila Mitchelle, but it bothered him that all of them had just disappeared from the face of the earth as if they had never been here in the first place. And the people he had actually known and cared about—well, he would miss them because they had made a difference in his life. Life seemed more precarious than ever. Life was something he had had to fight for year after year, and it was also something he could easily lose at any moment.

James grew more and more despondent. He became paranoid about life and nervous that if he didn't take extra precautions something would happen. He might get run over while crossing the street as soon as he set foot off the curb. He might get run over even if he was crossing with a green light. He might have a fatal accident while driving. Something might fall on him— a branch from a tree, a steel beam from a building—who knew? Death lurked around every corner, though curiously he toyed with and dared it. He took to driving extremely fast—ninety or a hundred miles an hour—along country roads. He drove recklessly, and though he didn't want anyone else to be injured, he apparently wanted to test the possibility himself. One afternoon, in the midst of an alcoholic binge, he drunkenly admitted to me that it was not uncommon for him to walk downtown to bridges that spanned Rock Creek Park or the Potomac River, stand at the railing in the middle, and watch below while wondering if he might dare jump. He said that he was often tempted to jump, and I believed him. He told me that there were some days he felt that the only way he would ever find peace would be by dying—and I believed him then, too. I knew that my father was convinced that he had only days to live and that he saw each night as the end of one day less to live his life.

By early June, James had become so severely depressed and uncharacteristically lethargic that he couldn't work. He stopped taking his daily seven-mile walks, lost his appetite, had trouble sleeping, and emphatically didn't want to be social. When Ruth suggested going to a dinner party, he would refuse. When his girlfriend dropped by, he didn't want to see her. And though the birth of Jenniemae's baby girl had been a nice break in a difficult string of months, it was not going to pull him out of this depression.

Depression was not altogether new for James. On and off throughout his life he had battled that feeling, a sinking, dark gloominess. Sometimes he had been able to get through it by working or being with friends. Sometimes he got through a dark period by finding a new lover or buying a new gadget or designing a new suit. But this time he felt locked in his own mind and he couldn't find a way out.

When James fell into what my mother frequently called a "period"—a term I always thought strange since a period seemed to signify the end of something rather than the beginning of it—there was an unwritten rule in the house that he should not be bothered. It was clear that he did not want our advice or our help. He just wanted to be left alone, and we knew it. Usually he would disappear by holing up in his office for hours every day. Sometimes he would remain there the entire day and into the night, only leaving when the rest of the house was asleep. The clear message was that he didn't want to speak to anyone at all.

It is difficult to entirely disappear in a house filled with other people coming and going, however. Even though he tried to hunker down in complete privacy, pieces of his dark world would overflow into the rest of the house. For instance, occasionally he would write notes to himself on scraps of paper and then accidentally—or was it on purpose?—leave one on the bathroom sink or on the kitchen counter. The notes seemed to be reminders of what he should be doing or thinking. One might be a shopping list of things he would like to have if he were living an ordinary life—like cottage cheese, English muffins, apples, Edam cheese, yellow legal pads, envelopes. Another scrap of paper might have a quote, such as one from Dostoevsky, "To be conscious is an illness—a real thorough-going illness."

James had one constant companion during this time: I. W. Harper. He had bottles of bourbon that he kept in his office closet "just in case," and this spring was a "just in case" time. Usually compulsively meticulous, he now allowed his office to become a complete mess, filled with empty bottles, ashtrays overflowing with cigarette butts, papers on the floor, and books stacked everywhere. Side by side against the back wall stood unopened brown cardboard boxes of books, the ones sent from *Scientific American* that he was supposed to review. Next to the boxes stood stacks of six or seven books James had already read and needed to review. Usually after books were reviewed, an assistant would catalog them and put them on shelves. It was almost a daily ritual of James's: Open the boxes, read the books, review them, and have them cataloged; open, read, review, and catalog.

Years before he had hired a librarian—Marianna—who still came to the house to catalog these books. She would fill out an index card for each new book, listing the author, title, and publication date, place the cards alphabetically in a metal file cabinet, and then put the books on the appropriate shelves. If anyone, either family or friends, wanted to read a book, he or she had to first ask James, and once he said yes, the book could be checked out on a card. As soon as the book was returned, the card was replaced and the book put back on the proper shelf. By 1955, James's library contained well over forty thousand books. Keeping those books safe and in order was very much in sync with his exacting personality. Now, however, Marianna was not allowed into his office.

After a week at this low ebb, James began to have severe chest pains. He mentioned this to Ruth, but since he tended toward hypochondria anyway, she chose to ignore the symptoms this time. Sometimes she listened to his complaints and other times she did not. The pains might truly signify danger and they might not. It was difficult for her to know when to take a complaint—a chest pain—seriously, and more often than not, when the two were not getting along well, it was unlikely that Ruth would take the time to listen about James's chest pain. And this was one of those times.

This time James felt worse than usual. His stomach was upset and the pain that usually circled the middle of his chest now radiated from his chest over and down through his left arm. Curiously, the worse the pain became, the less anxious he was. What should have been an alarm sounding became a dull hum. He realized that there was a good possibility he was having a heart attack and yet, unlike other times this had happened, he had no inclination to do anything about it. He was dispirited, melancholy, and exhausted. He seemed to have lost his will or desire to live.

Our house was often filled with lies and pretense. There were times when we all acted as though what was going on wasn't going on—but it actually *was* going on. This was a family affair that we all participated in since it takes more than one to make a real lie work; one person tells it and the others have to believe it, or behave as though they do.

James was depressed and slowly killing himself with alcohol and cigarettes and anxiety, and the rest of the family was pretending it wasn't happening. James might be having a heart attack but we all pretended otherwise. It wasn't that we didn't care; it was that we weren't supposed to interfere and we were supposed to believe—or at least hope—that pretending a thing could make it so. It was a family habit to pretend and therefore we all thought we were doing what was "right." Habits like this one have a way of seeming like the best course of action to take just because they have been done time and again. Like driving through a red light or drinking one too many drinks every evening, the more often you do it, the more you believe it is acceptable.

There was just one person who wouldn't play the game: Jenniemae. And while she allowed this dire state of affairs to go on for a week, she wasn't pretending, she was simply following rules. But after more than a week of allowing the family rules to preside, she wanted to cut through the nonsense.

"This has gone on long 'nough," she told me one morning. "Somethin' has to change. Pretendin' a thing is bad luck. Jaybird don't rob his own nest. And in case you don't get what I am sayin', it is plain and clear: Pretendin' is like robbin' your own nest."

"Why?"

"Because if you go and pretend a thing is or isn't so, then pieces of flesh get ripped from your own body while you're not payin' attention to what needs attention paid."

"How does that happen?" I asked her.

"I'll tell you. Pretendin' eats at a man, sucks his bones dry. It first takes the soul out of a man, then it turns around and plucks out his eyes to make him blind. It'll kill you but it'll kill you slowly, which is worse than a quick dyin'. Pretendin' is bad luck."

Jenniemae had told me about a number of things that were bad luck: "It is bad luck to step over a person if he is sleepin'. It is bad luck to put your clothes on inside out. It is bad luck when a hen crows like a rooster. It is bad luck to turn back once you leave on a journey." But pretending was about as bad as bad luck could get.

So although Jenniemae did not feel it was appropriate for her to interfere and break the rules, she wasn't about to sit around and pretend a thing wasn't so when in fact it *was* so. She had watched as Mister James hid out in his office. She had witnessed his not once coming out for meals or walks or talks. And while she thought it would just end on its own and whatever was bothering him would disappear—it didn't disappear. For Jenniemae, James was no different from a blind man lost in the thick woods except that Mister James was lost in his own house and lost in his own head.

It was close to June 16—Missus Ruth's birthday—and Jenniemae liked birthdays. This was no time for everyone in the house to be so down on themselves. Days before Ruth's birthday,

Jenniemae decided that it was time to end the nonsense. When only she and Mister James were home, she resolutely climbed the stairs to the second floor and knocked on his office door. When there was no response, she tried the door handle and found it locked. Staring at the door, she asked, "Mister James? You in there?" There was still no response, so she tried again. "Now, Mister James, you are in there. I know it and I would like for you to say somethin'." Still she got no response. More forcefully then, she said, "Mister James, you open this here door now. It's me, Jenniemae, and I ain't goin' nowhere till you open this here door. You hear me now?" She waited. It took a few minutes before James finally opened the door. Jenniemae took one look at him and was shocked.

"My Lord now," she said, looking at his pale, disheveled, drunken appearance. "You look like one ugly dead thing or another. What is this that happened to you?"

James said nothing but sat back down in his chair amidst the books, papers, and empty bottles of I. W. Harper.

"Lord, you made some mess here. Lord have mercy." She shook her head.

James rested his head upon his forearm on the desk.

"Lord. You okay?"

He shook his head slowly.

"Mus' be bad, then, huh?"

James was silent.

"When a man finds hisself under the water, he has got to kick to get to the top. You know what I am sayin'?"

He didn't answer.

"I know what it is to be under, Mister James, and I know what it is to want to stop all the kickin' forever . . . but listen here—if you stop kickin', you can't change back your mind. Once the kickin' stops, then it's over and done. Over and done." Jenniemae paused and then said, "Mister James, it's not your time to go. It's not your time. I am tellin' you that right now because I know it. So you better start kickin'."

James still said nothing. His facial muscles tightened and he grew suddenly more ashen than he already had been.

Jenniemae was frightened by the change in his coloring. "Mister James. You okay here?"

He didn't respond.

"You don't look so good."

He didn't move.

"Lord. This is bad. We got to get you to your doctor. Lord, now you have to ease up on yo'self. I'm goin' to call for help. You hear me now? I'm callin' for help."

Jenniemae reached for the telephone receiver and dialed 0 for the operator. When a woman's voice came on the line, Jenniemae told her that she had to have an ambulance come right away. "Right away now, you hear me? I work for Mister James and he is very sick. . . . Yes . . . No . . . We are at . . . ," and Jenniemae gave the operator the address. After going back and forth with the address, it is my guess that the operator assumed it was a white man's home. Otherwise, it would have been likely no ambulance would have been sent.

Half an hour later an ambulance siren could be heard. "It's almost here. You're gonna be all right now, Mister James. You're gonna be all right," Jenniemae said, standing next to James and rubbing his neck and his back as he lay slumped over on his desk.

"Oh Lord," she repeated. "Oh Lord."

Then he said softly, "They're crooks."

"Who? Who are crooks?"

"They are."

"Who are we talkin' about?"

"Them," he said.

"The ambulance men? They're not crooks. What are you talkin' about?"

"They just come to steal your body and then they take your soul," he said.

"No sir. That's not right," she told him.

"But it is right. They stick one needle in here and another one in there, and next thing you know, they own you . . . you're in their grips—no body, no soul."

"Mister James, that's crazy talk."

"No it isn't."

"Ain't no one can take your soul. They can take your body, but there ain't no one that can take your soul."

"You sure of that?" he asked, and even smiled.

"I am sure."

"You going to watch them?" he asked.

"I'll watch everythin' they do."

"And how will you know if they take my soul?" he asked.

"Because a man without a soul has nothing in the back of his eyes," Jenniemae told him.

"And you can see there?"

"I can. Now, don't you worry. I ain't lettin' them take no more than this here broken-up body."

After a moment he asked her, "You think I'm gonna die, Jenniemae?"

"No. Not your time. Not your time yet. I can see that in your eyes, too. Death is in a man's eyes before it hits his heart . . . and it ain't there," she said, and the sirens stopped as the ambulance pulled up the long driveway.

"You know what they say, Jenniemae."

"No, I don't know. What do they say?"

"Man works hard all his life and the Lord laughs at all that work."

"And what's that supposed to mean, Mister James?"

"Your Lord—He's laughing at me now. Spent all that time working so hard and what's the point?"

"Point is that you do good work with His numbers, Mister James. The Lord is not laughin' at you. No sir, He's not. He knows that someone has to work out all those numbers and put them in a proper place."

"Proper place?"

"That's right," she said.

"What I do is just gambling with numbers. That's what I do. I gamble numbers just like you do. I bet on them going one way or another and hope they work out. Sometimes I win and sometimes I lose," he said despondently.

"I don't gamble. I dream."

"I don't dream. I gamble."

"Lord, Mister James. You just quiet down now."

# CHAPTER SEVENTEEN

*"Trouble is what troubles."*

When the paramedics arrived and brought the stretcher into the office, they told Jenniemae to leave the room, but James demanded that she stay. "I want her here," he told them. When they said there wasn't enough room for her to stay, James insisted, "There's room."

Jenniemae stood absolutely still in the corner of the office while they loaded James onto the stretcher and gave him a shot of morphine to ease his pain. As they carried him out of the room, he looked back at Jenniemae and said, "Told you. The needles."

"Now, don't you worry, Mister James. I'm watchin' and you're goin' to be fine. You hear me now. You are goin' to be jus' fine."

He looked at her sadly and it was all Jenniemae could do to keep from breaking down in tears. Mister James looked tired, pale, and weak—she had never seen him look like this before. Whatever assurances she might give him, she wasn't quite convinced that everything *would* turn out all right. Maybe he would die, and if he did, then—well, she didn't want to even think about that. There could be no "if he did's." She had to think positively. She had to concentrate on his returning to health. There were no two ways about that. Jenniemae watched as the paramedics negotiated the stairs, making sure that the stretcher carrying James didn't tilt or sway. She watched as they walked out the front door and the stretcher disappeared, with Mister James lying perfectly still on it. Was he alive?

Jenniemae stood absolutely still at the top of the stairway, waiting for she didn't know what exactly. Her feet didn't want to take her down the stairs, back into his office, or anywhere else. They just wanted to stand right where they were standing. She stood there listening to the sounds of the paramedics carrying James to the ambulance. She barely took a breath as she listened to them talking with each other as if there was no patient in a stretcher between them. She could have sworn that they were talking about a baseball game—something like that. Was it possible that Mister James had already passed away and the paramedics were talking about baseball as if nothing had happened here? Or was it possible that he was hanging on and they were discussing baseball, not caring about the man on the stretcher's well-being? Jenniemae was wound as tight as she ever had been wound, and listening to these paramedics made her feel sick to her stomach. "Lord, please. Please," she said quietly to herself.

Jenniemae heard the back doors to the ambulance close and the driver's door slam shut. She remained standing at the top stair. And then she heard the engine start up and the ambulance back out of the driveway, and as soon as it headed down the street, the driver put on his sirens and sped away. Then and only then did Jenniemae move. She sat down on the top step of the staircase, put her head in her hands, and began to cry. "Lord, oh Lord, have mercy," she said as tears ran down her cheeks.

# CHAPTER EIGHTEEN

*"Pig knows what tree to rub up against."*

James was taken to George Washington University Hospital. He had had a heart attack. He had sustained more damage to his already weakened heart muscle, but he was alive. He had not had a stroke and neither his speech nor his physical movement was impaired. The doctors continued to monitor him with EKG's and blood tests, but beyond that there was nothing more to be done. He would remain in the hospital for ten days.

The morning following James's heart attack, Jenniemae arrived at work earlier than usual. She had spent most of the night awake and worried, so she had decided to come in early. She wanted to be closer to the house, to the family. At least if she were in the house, she could find out what was going on with Mister James. She could ask questions or overhear conversations. There was no thought of her visiting the hospital. That would never have entered her mind, but she did want to know how Mister James was doing. While in the kitchen she could hear Ruth talking on the telephone upstairs.

As soon as Ruth came downstairs, Jenniemae asked, "Missus Ruth, is Mister James all right today? Is he going to be all right?"

"I think so, Jenniemae. And I want to thank you for calling the operator and getting help yesterday."

Jenniemae thought for a moment before responding. "He didn't look right at all, Missus Ruth. You would have done it, too, right away."

"Yes, I'm sure he looked horrible. But I think he's going to be okay and hopefully he'll return home soon."

"Do you think so?"

"Yes."

"Please be sure and tell me how he's doin'—can you do that please?"

"Certainly I will."

Though Jenniemae went about her work, her mind was pre-occupied all that day. And the following morning Jenniemae asked, "How's he doin' today, Missus Ruth?"

"Better, Jenniemae. Better, thank you."

"You think he'll be comin' home soon?"

"I hope so."

"You tell him I am prayin' for him every night and every day."

"I will, Jenniemae."

Jenniemae didn't like the emptiness of the house—it wasn't the same at all when Mister James wasn't home. One after-noon, about a week after the heart attack, I was sitting in the kitchen with Jenniemae and she asked, "Can you call him on the telephone?"

"Call him?"

"Yes. Can you do that?"

"Really? I don't think they allow children to call the hospital."

"How do you know that for sure?" Jenniemae asked.

"Because Mother said I couldn't visit since children under twelve aren't allowed in the patients' rooms, so I figure I wouldn't be allowed to call, either."

"But they don't know you're only ten when you're calling," she said.

I was surprised that Jenniemae might be asking me to do something that was against the rules. "But they might know."

"How could they know? You just have to disguise yourself."

"What do you mean, disguise myself?"

"You got to sound older. That's easy 'nough. You can do that plenty easy," she said.

"But I'm not allowed—" I started to say, and she interrupted by telling me that there was such a thing as "allowed" and then there was another thing she called "should be allowed."

"Is this a 'should be allowed'?" I asked, relishing the notion that Jenniemae was asking me to do something against the rules, which was already something, unbeknownst to her, I was accustomed to doing. By the time I was ten, stealing, skipping school, and hiding out had become an ingrained part of my personality: I commonly broke rules, from crossing the street on a red light to getting kicked out of the Girl Scouts for refusing to say the Pledge of Allegiance. Now, having Jenniemae's approval to break a rule seemed better than many things I could have imagined. "Are you sure?" I asked her again. She nodded.

"You got to pretend to be older when you talk to the operator at the hospital. You understand? Just pretend. Just think on it."

"How?" I asked.

"Imagine older in your mind. Imagine that you're an older person—say a girl who is sixteen. A big girl like that. You imagine a sixteen-year-old girl and then you imagine what she would be saying. Imagine the words and then imagine your older voice. Make it lower . . . and then you'll be jus' fine. A person can imagine a thing and make it his own," she suggested.

"Well . . . okay." I thought about this for a moment and figured it could be done. After all, it wasn't a stretch for me to believe I was more than one person—the secret one and the "other" one. I telephoned the switchboard at George Washington University Hospital. I lowered my voice and asked to speak to Mr. James Newman. There was a silence on the other end of the line and I thought I had failed and something terrible might happen. Would they arrest me? Minutes passed as I held that telephone receiver. Jenniemae, who almost always looked calm, now also looked nervous. Then I heard a few clicks and a woman came back on the line and said, "Just hold here." I waited a bit longer before I heard my father's voice.

"Hello," he said softly.

"Is that you?" I asked.

"Seems so," he said, and I could see right through the black telephone receiver that my father was smiling. Jenniemae, too, was grinning as she watched me speaking to him.

"It's me and it's Jenniemae here. We're calling you even though we're not supposed to," I told him.

He laughed. "Good for you."

"They thought I was older. Jenniemae taught me how to do that."

"Good job, then. You did well."

"How are you? Can you come home soon?"

"I'm pretty good and hopefully I'll be home at the end of the week."

"Do you want to say hello to Jenniemae?"

"Sure I do," he said.

But Jenniemae stepped back a few paces. "Oh no, I can't do that," she said. I insisted.

"Come on," I kept saying. "He wants to say hello."

Finally she took hold of the receiver and said, "Mister James, that you there?"

"Hi, Jenniemae. It's me. Same me."

"Better not be the same you." She smiled and tears welled in her eyes.

"It is," he told her, and chuckled.

"Well, you come home soon now. You hear me?"

"I hear you."


On the day before James was to be released from the hospital, Ruth told Jenniemae that they needed to change the angle of his bed and a carpenter would be coming by to lift the head of the bed higher than the foot. The doctors had suggested that this was important for his circulation. Then, she gave Jenniemae a list of the things James could eat and those he couldn't. Although Jenniemae could recognize numbers and some words she had seen time and again, she surely couldn't read all the words on that list—particularly the new words. Not wanting to admit she didn't know those words, Jenniemae took the piece of paper, carefully folded it, and put it in her pocket.

*Oh Lord,* she thought to herself. *What am I gonna do with this?*

# CHAPTER NINETEEN

*"You can hide a fire, but what do you do with the smoke?"*

After ten days James came home from the hospital. Ruth picked him up in the morning. He hated the way she drove and complained all the way home about it.

"You don't hold the steering wheel like that. Ten and two, ten and two. That's where you put your hands."

"Fine, fine." She didn't want to argue.

"Put your turn signal on or put your arm out to tell when you're turning. You can't just turn whenever you want without signaling."

"Fine, fine. I will."

"Pump the brakes, don't slam them down."

"Jesus, I should have left you in the hospital. Stop complaining," Ruth finally said. "You're going to have another heart attack."

"I'm not sure which is a worse way to go—a heart attack or being driven to my death by you at the wheel."

•   •   •

Jenniemae had been nervous all morning, anticipating Mister James's arrival. There was so much to do that she almost wished that Serena had not been let go after Lila Belle's birth—almost. Jenniemae had spent the morning cleaning, dusting, re-cleaning, re-dusting, making his bed—the headboard now raised—straightening his room, washing the windows, dusting the window blinds and windowsills. She wanted to make sure that while lying in bed he could easily look out at the dogwood trees, now adorned with their delicate white blossoms, and beyond the dogwoods he would be able to see the leaves that were blooming on the maple and oak trees. She hoped that when he got out of the car he would notice that along the front walkway the pink and white azalea bushes had blossomed and between those bushes there were delicate purple violets. For Jenniemae it would be a sign of his returning to health if he took notice of spring. *Now, Mister James can't break that plow point twice*, she thought.

"Breaking the plow point twice" meant doing something again that had either failed or was stupid the first time around. Breaking the plow point twice was something she did if she bet on the same losing number more than once, overcooked the roast beef again, spilled a glass of water more than once, or dropped the sweeper on her foot twice in the same day. Having a heart attack once was a bad, bad thing, but having it twice was playing with the devil. Having a heart attack more than once was breaking the plow point twice.

Jenniemae had cleaned compulsively all morning not only to make the house look perfect for Mister James's arrival but also to help take her mind off that list Missus Ruth had given her the

day before. The list was, as she had been told, the hospital di-
etary requirements that Mister James had to have. That unread
folded piece of paper still tucked in her pocket was important.
She hadn't yet decided how to handle the situation. She would
like to have ordered a delivery of everything on that list, but she
couldn't read it. She was going to have to depend on common
sense and figure out on her own what was good for Mister
James to eat. So she did just that. She placed her order at the
local farmer's market for all the good things she thought he
should have. She ordered salad greens and red peppers, green
peppers and string beans, sweet peas and apples, oranges and
bananas and peaches that were in season. She ordered melba
toast, English muffins, and strawberry jam because she knew he
liked them. And she ordered oatmeal and tea, and chickens to
roast and steaks to broil.

Jenniemae was stubborn. She was not self-righteous but she
was definitely stubborn, and when it came to certain issues, like
what was healthy to eat or what numbers to play or how to treat
another person, she was absolutely 100 percent certain she was
right. "Can't tell a black snake which way to get to the hen's
nest—'cause he knows." Jenniemae knew what she knew. But
just in case she might have missed an item or two—and for an
added sense of security—ever since Missus Ruth had handed
her that piece of paper with the list on it, she carried it around,
folded up neatly, in her pocket. There was, in her mind, an outside chance that the information just might burn its way
through the pocket and into her mind, which would guarantee
her accuracy.

When Ruth brought James home, Jenniemae watched from the kitchen window as the car pulled up and stopped before the closed garage door. Ruth got out of the driver's side and stood waiting for her husband to get out of his side. Jenniemae heard Ruth say, "Do you need help?" and though she didn't hear James respond, she assumed he had since Ruth didn't walk around the car to open his door. James sat in the car, staring at the closed garage door for what seemed like a long time before opening his door. Jenniemae was concerned. Did he need help? Was he going to be okay? Was he going to be different? Or himself?

James slowly got out of the car. He stood up, stretched his arms, and then looked around for a moment—it seemed to Jenniemae that he was taking notes about where he was and the way things looked. Wasn't he sure where he was? Or did he just want to reconnect slowly? Then she noticed a slight smile come over his face and he began to slowly walk along the path leading to the back door. Jenniemae opened the back door and held it open. When he came close she smiled and said, "My, my, Mister James, don't you look yourself now."

"Well, thank you, Jenniemae. I hope to be back to myself soon. Not quite there yet."

"Looking mighty good, though," she lied. Jenniemae hadn't known what to expect, but what she saw now was not easy. She had never seen James look so pale or walk so slowly. He had lost weight—his clothes hung on his body as if he had borrowed them from a heavier man—and when he walked through the door and into the kitchen, Jenniemae thought that he looked fifteen years older than he had a week before.

"You lookin' good, Mister James," she lied again.

"And now you are truly doing a bad job of lying," he said with a smile.

"Well, you look good to me, Mister James," she said, smiling back.

"Then you're blind and a liar." He smiled again, thanked her, and said he was delighted to be home. "They were trying to kill me with that hospital food," he told her.

"Is that so? What would you like to eat, Mister James?"

"Well, now, what would I like?" he mused. "I would like a rare roast beef sandwich with tomato, lettuce, mustard, and mayonnaise and some of your homemade country fried potatoes on the side and then perhaps a bowl of ice cream with hot chocolate sauce for dessert. That is what I would like. However, that is not what I can have," he told her.

She laughed. "I know that's not what you s'pposed to have."

"Let's settle for a cup of tea and maybe a salad with some melba toast. Does that sound all right with you?"

"Yes, mighty all right, and I have got that here."

"Ruth said she gave you a list that the hospital put together, but you don't need that list because I can tell you what I like and I know what's good for me," James said, aware that she probably could not recognize all the words on that list. It was curious to James that his wife had never noticed that fact. In the seven years that Jenniemae had worked for them she had found a way to fool Ruth and get by without having to read—but for James it had been obvious from the start. She couldn't read recipes and made them up as she went along; she couldn't read laundry instructions and made do just as well without them; she couldn't read everything on Ruth's grocery lists but found ways around that by asking enough questions about what Ruth wanted for dinner to get by. When these strategies failed to solve the problem, Jenniemae usually asked the handyman and gardener, Mr. Elton Harris, who worked at the house three or four days a week. When sober, Mr. Harris, as he was called by everyone, would read the lists and notes to Jenniemae.

"Says here you got to get six sweet potatoes, a pound of lima beans, one roast pork, fresh tarragon, basil, and some butter. Now, can you remember all of that?" He would read the list once more and she would memorize what she needed to order from the grocery store.

But Mr. Harris had been drunk almost the entire ten days that Mister James had been gone, and Jenniemae hated to be around that stinking man when he was drunk. He was two people—one was a nice, gentle, helpful man, and the other was a mean and dangerous drunk—and when he was the drunk man, she kept her distance. She found dealing with Mr. Harris problematic. On the one hand, he was needed around the house, and on the other, she thought he had an evil streak and couldn't be trusted. She said there were many reasons for Mr. Harris's being so disagreeable, the most important of which was that he had been called "boy" once too often in his lifetime. "If people go and call a man 'boy' all the time and they are meanin' by 'boy' that the man is a no-good nothing of a person," Jenniemae said, "well, Lord knows that that man is goin' to listen to that talk once too often and that man will be becomin' what he is being called. It is a miserable way of makin' a good man into a nothing of a man. You can't be callin' a man a boy if you want that man to be a man."

Mr. Harris—sober or drunk—was a talented gardener who took pride in his work. He chose which flowers to plant where and when, tended the flower beds, pruned and cared for the azalea bushes, the hydrangeas, the violets, the tulips, and the rosebushes. He made things grow that had never grown in the neighborhood before. We had a peach tree in the backyard and an apricot tree, an apple tree and a fig tree. He planted lettuce, carrots, radishes, tomatoes, and quite a few corn stalks. Mr. Harris nurtured the grass and trimmed the hedges, cared for the dogwoods on the hillside so that their white spring blossoms looked like a fresh bridal veil. He tended to the cherry trees so carefully that their pink flowers that blossomed every April looked like delicate ballet slippers, each one made especially for a particular branch. Every spring he designed something new for the flower beds that lined the walkway to the house. That spring he had planted pink and white impatiens amid the tiny purple violets. In the autumn he diligently raked the leaves and planted new tulip bulbs. Toward the end of March he had planted new rosebushes and added pink and white lilies, delphiniums, marigolds, petunias, multicolored pansies, and little purple violets that were speckled with orange or yellow centers. Mr. Harris could have worked the gardens of Versailles; he was that skillful. He selected the seeds carefully and would drive miles out to special nurseries in Virginia to purchase better seeds than he could find closer to home. He weeded, watered, fertilized, and cared for each plant singularly as if it were his child. I couldn't understand how such a man, who was so careful and gentle with flowers, could also be what Jenniemae claimed he was—an evil man who murdered his wife one night. She said it had happened but nothing would ever come of it because that was the way it was. The police weren't likely to care if there was one less poor Negro woman living in southeast D.C. "There are two ways to live," Jenniemae said. "One way is the way we live across town and the other way is the way it is here."

So Jenniemae only turned to Mr. Harris when she had no alternative. But this time she couldn't even do that because he was on a drinking binge. She began to explain to Mister James, "Missus Ruth, she did give me that list and I was—" when he interrupted.

"Jenniemae, don't worry about it."

"Well, I do. Worry is what I do most times. I worry, whether or not it is about that list or you lyin' sick in the hospital or a whole host of things. I know a thing or two about worryin'."

"I know. And I have to apologize for all of that. Next time I won't have a heart attack in front of you," he said with a laugh.

"Now, that is not one bit funny. Not funny at all," she said sternly.

"I know it's not funny, but I am sorry for making you have to go through all of that."

"You don't have to be sorry."

"How about this. I'll stop being sorry if you'll let me show you how to read just a few of the words on that list. Don't say no before you think a minute. Some of those words are hard, so it's nothing to be ashamed about if you don't know them," he said, allowing her to pretend she could read some of the words.

Jenniemae stared at him for a moment before answering. "Well," she said, and stopped. "Well, to tell you the truth, I can't read most of 'em!"

"I know. Let's just call it a favor I can do for you."

"All right, then. One favor for another," she said.

The list became the first thing that Jenniemae learned how to read. Over the next weeks she learned the words *tea, no butter, no cream, melba toast, apples, grapefruit, lox, cottage cheese, carrots,* and many others that had been on that list, as well as some that hadn't been there. James taught her to read by memorizing the words and then by sounding them out. It may not have been the way they taught reading in school, but it seemed to work.

"*Butter.* That word is *butter.* Just look at it and picture it in your mind. Take a photograph of it for your mind and then remember what it looks like. And one more thing, Jenniemae . . . I'm not supposed to have butter."

"No butter?"

"And no cream."

"Is that right?"

"That's it. No butter. No cream. The word *no* is an important word to learn to read."

"I got it. I know that one already. Many a time be."

"And then there is *yes.*"

"I know that one, too. *No, yes*—I got. *Butter,* I got, too, now."

"Okay then. *No, yes,* and *butter* are a few of the most important words in the English language. So you've got all three. Excellent."

"Okay. I got the new *butter* now settlin' in my mind . . . it's in there now."

"All right. Here's the word *cabbage*. See it and photograph it and set it in your mind . . . and you can soon forget it because I hate cabbage."

"Okay, then. I got *cabbage*. I got it. I know to forget it and I got *no butter* and I got *no cream*."

"The next time you see these words on your list or written, you'll know what it says and what you want to do."

"Sure thing, then. What's the next word?"

"How about *coffee?*"

"Yes, that's a good word. I need that word. And show me how the word *tea* is written down, because I know you like your tea."

"All right. Here it is: *tea.* T-e-a. Just like that."

"Okay, then," she said.

Over the next days Jenniemae set ten or more words into her memory. It became a game for her—like playing the numbers. She loved learning new words almost as much as she loved playing those numbers.

After a couple of weeks James said, "Once you can read the words over and over, then you can start to copy them down yourself with a pen and a piece of paper."

"Is that so . . . Lord have mercy . . . I'll be writing my own lists," she said, smiling.

"Yes you will."

"Can you show me how to read and write *Lila* on a fresh piece of paper?"

And James took out a clean piece of paper and wrote down *Lila*. "Look here. Just copy the words down with the pen as you see them. Write the letters under the ones I have written here and you will have written your daughter's name."

Jenniemae took the pen and did as he had told her. She wrote L-i-l-a.

Then he showed her how to write *Jenniemae Harrington*.

"That's somethin' . . . ain't it?" she said proudly.

"Indeed it is something."

"I like that. I like writing that. Maybe you can teach me to write a prayer. How about you teach me that?"

"Never going to happen," he laughed. "Not now, not ever."

"Lord, Mister James, it would do you some good to write one down yo'self."

"I doubt it. You can't ask for help if you don't believe. It's just part of the game."

"Lord . . ."

"I've got you to help me out. I don't need to pray."

"Lord, Lord. Rat eats the sugar cane, the innocent lizard dies for it."

# CHAPTER TWENTY

*"Put your heart at ease."*

On April 2, 1956, the soap opera *As the World Turns* had its debut. Set in the imaginary town of Oakdale, Illinois, it centered around the juicy and turbulent lives of the Hughes family. Helen Wagner played the role of Nancy Hughes and Don MacLaughlin played her husband, Chris Hughes. By 1955, half of the U.S. population owned televisions sets. People had already become accustomed to tuning into shows like *The Texaco Theater* with Milton Berle, *Camel News Caravan* with a cigarette-smoking John Cameron Swayze, *The Jack Benny Show, Amos and Andy*, and *Howdy Doody. As the World Turns* was a new format—a half-hour soap opera—and the show was aired during the afternoon in order to attract thousands of housewives who might like to see what was going on behind closed doors in their neighborhoods. The scheduled time, one-thirty P.M., was also when James broke from work and had lunch. He had recently purchased a Zenith round-screen television set boxed in a mahogany self-standing case, but our family only watched a few shows. Evenings were rarely spent watching television, and finding something interesting on during the middle of the day seemed highly unlikely. But James had read about this new soap opera making its premiere, and he was curious. He told Jenniemae that rather than eating his lunch in his office as usual, he would be having it in the den.

The den, whose walls were lined floor to ceiling with books, had two comfortable lounge chairs, a small coffee table, a twin-size bed—and the Zenith television set. James turned on the set before the scheduled show time because it took a few moments for the screen to warm up and come into focus. Before any recognizable picture came on the screen, a gray background would appear with broken black lines and thousands of small black dots. James stood before the television and waited for it to clear. When Jenniemae entered the room with his lunch tray, she, too, stood watching the screen.

"What is going to be on there?" she asked.

"It's a new show. I wanted to see what it would be like."

"Is that so? About what?"

"About a family."

"Is that right? And what do they do?"

"I don't know. We'll soon see."

And then the screen cleared and the music played. *As the World Turns* began and the Hughes family was introduced to James, Jenniemae, and anyone else who tuned into the soap opera that day.

The following day, April 3, James again tuned in to *As the World Turns*. Jenniemae did not stay for the entire program but

James did, and from then on, every single weekday James sat in one of the lounge chairs, with his lunch tray on the coffee table before him, and watched the saga of the Hughes family from Oakdale unravel. As unlikely as it was, James, who just an hour before might have been unraveling mathematical mysteries, working out the details of Goedel's Proof, or finishing a piece about Bertrand Russell and Alfred North Whitehead's *Principia Mathematica*, would now be giving his undivided attention to all the dramas on *As the World Turns*. It was a routine he followed religiously unless interrupted by something exceedingly important. If a girlfriend came around during the show, then she, too, had to watch quietly. If the telephone rang, he ignored it. And while Jenniemae did not usually watch the entire program, James would often fill her in with the details later in the afternoon. Stories of unwanted pregnancies, breakups, affairs, marriages, divorces, new jobs, deaths, and births were part of their conversation.

"Now, Mister James, you don't mean to tell me . . . that didn't happen . . . she couldn't do that!"

"Oh, but it did. She is seeing him on the side and doesn't know he's her lost uncle."

"No . . ."

"Oh, but yes," he would say, and laugh. He knew how absurd it all seemed, but he loved watching the show.

Jenniemae's take on why James liked to watch *As the World Turns* every day was that it put "his heart at ease."

# CHAPTER TWENTY-ONE

*"It's bad luck if a man's shadow falls*

*onto you while you're lyin' down.*

*It's good luck if that don't happen."*

Nineteen fifty-six was a year of turning points. In 1956 a young Negro girl named Autherine Lucy enrolled in the University of Alabama, sparking riots. The Supreme Court ruled that segregation in public transportation was unconstitutional and violence erupted. Ten Negroes entered Sturgis High School in Kentucky amid protests from whites. Elvis Presley performed on Ed Sullivan's television show *Toast of the Town* singing "Hound Dog" and "Love Me Tender," moving his hips in a most suggestive manner. The Soviets invaded Budapest to crush the Hungarian revolution, and thousands were killed.

And 1956 was a huge year in our house. Jenniemae said it was a good-luck year. It was a turning point for us because, for good or bad, money can change your life. And more often than not it does change your life.

That year the book James had been working on for fifteen years was finally published. *The World of Mathematics* was a four-volume, 2,469-page treatise on the history, philosophy, and science of mathematics. *The New York Times* said it was "the most amazing selection of articles about mathematics yet published . . . a delight to readers with a wide range of backgrounds." Fortuitously, *The World of Mathematics* came out at the same time Americans had become seriously concerned with the poor quality of the country's science and math education, particularly in light of the Soviet Union's progress in these fields. The Soviets were better educated in the sciences and in mathematics, and it was rumored that they were about to be the first to launch a satellite to orbit the earth. There was a widely held belief by educators, scientists, and politicians, a belief fostered by the media, that should the Soviets achieve greater successes in the space race and gain momentum in that sphere, they would surely be able to control the new global economic and political playing fields. It became imperative that the United States immediately overhaul its failing math and science programs across the country, from the very earliest years in school.

Timing and luck can mean everything in business endeavors, including publishing. For a decade and a half James had been working on this definitive work on mathematics. Had it come out ten years earlier, or five, or even one year earlier, it might have been a sleeper. But luckily, 1956 was just the right time. No book of this magnitude on the subject of mathematics had ever been published. For years his publishers had been second-guessing themselves, wondering, first, whether Newman would ever finish the project (which seemed doubtful to them) and, second, who would buy such a large book on any subject, much less on mathematics. "He'll be dead before completing it," they joked at a board meeting led by Max Schuster of Simon &

Schuster. They didn't worry much about the five hundred dollars advance they'd paid him in 1942. If the book failed, the advance would be a tax write-off. When they considered the money brought in by their bestsellers, like *The New York Times Crossword Puzzle Book, The Best Crosswords Ever*, Will and Ariel Durant's *Story of Civilization*, and Bertrand Russell's *Philosophy of the World*, five hundred dollars lost on a book about mathematics that might never be completed, or might never be read even if it was, was nothing to keep one up at night over.

So *The World of Mathematics* was published in the fall of 1956 with little fanfare, but much to the surprise of everyone, it soon hit the bestseller list and stayed there for many months. Besides bringing James enormous pride for the work he'd completed, it afforded him a more prominent name and paid him large sums of money. He earned more money than he had ever imagined possible. Besides selling well in the United States, the book sold well in many other countries as well. James received job offers from well-known universities, he was in demand as a lecturer, and he became the first person ever to host a televised educational show on mathematics. He appeared on the two-year-old National Educational Television (NET) network, standing in front of a blackboard, where he lectured about various mathematical subjects ranging from puzzles to paradoxes, quantum mathematics to the theory of relativity, calculus to the history and philosophy behind number theory.

One of the first purchases James made with his new money was a newer, bigger house in Chevy Chase, Maryland. For my brother and me, it meant a change of schools and friends. For Jenniemae, it meant a longer ride from her home to our home—and it meant working for rich white folks instead of middle-class white folks. For James, it meant the opportunity to purchase certain material things he had never dreamed of owning. He loved fast, expensive cars. He loved driving by himself—sitting in the driver's seat and taking his mind off everything else by shifting, steering, watching the road, studying the tachometer, speedometer, and odometer, enjoying the curves and hills of a rural road and the stoplights and hustle of traffic of a congested city street. A car was a place of solace. A car was about speed and the ability to control—or to lose control. So he bought cars, and more cars.

James took the ownership of his new race cars seriously. He bought books and manuals to learn about each: its history, how big the engine was, what innovations had been made, how many of each model were in production, how fast it could go, and how long it took to go from zero to sixty miles per hour. He loved owning a wonderfully made machine that could be driven at over a hundred miles per hour. He became obsessed with different makes and studied the Jaguar, the Maserati, the Ferrari, the Lotus, the MG, the Aston Martin, and the Lamborghini. Not too long after he had deposited his first large royalty check, he ordered a racing green DB4, Series 1 Aston Martin from London. The DB4 was a six-cylinder, alloy block and head. It had coil-spring suspension, rack-and-pinion steering, Dunlop disc brakes, and a maximum speed of 140 miles per hour. There were only 149 of this Series 1 Aston Martin being built, and though the first one would not come off the assembly line until October of 1958, he considered the wait well worth it. In the meantime he ordered a silver French racing car with a Chrysler engine called a Facel Vega. Soon after the Facel Vega arrived, he bought a black Ford Thunderbird. He had always wanted to drive a Rolls-Royce, so within months he also bought one of them in midnight blue. And since he alone would be permitted to drive these cars, he bought a fifth car for Ruth to drive, a red Buick station wagon.

By the time all five cars were delivered, James had hired a construction company to build a three-car garage for the Aston Martin, the Facel Vega, and the midnight-blue Rolls. The Thunderbird and the Buick were to be left outside to withstand the elements. Choices had to be made daily about which car to drive. Generally, however, he drove the Aston Martin on sunny days, driving into the Maryland or Virginia countryside, cranking it up to frightening speeds and returning to relate just how fast he had gone. Pushing the Aston to speeds over a hundred miles per hour was commonplace, but his goal was getting it to 110 or 115. Once he even clocked his speed at 129 miles per hour. When bored with the Aston Martin, he drove the Facel Vega, when the Facel Vega and Aston Martin didn't suit the day, he took the Thunderbird. The Rolls he saved for special occasions, like going downtown for an appointment or taking the family to the D.C. ice-skating rink on Sunday mornings. Going to dinner parties or special political galas usually required arriving in the Aston Martin because that car—an English racing car—suggested edginess, speed, uniqueness. The Rolls was for different implications: It suggested success, wealth, and a sense of being beyond reproach.

While the Aston Martin cried out *speed*, the Rolls-Royce demanded *attention*. It was a work of art. It combined James's appreciation of design and style, his need for perfection, and his perverse sense of humor all in one. He particularly enjoyed certain features, such as the backseat cherrywood writing table, the fold-out bar, the window that separated the driver from the passengers, and the pearl-inlaid steering wheel. The Rolls was a car for dignitaries to be driven from event to event by handsomely dressed chauffeurs wearing white gloves and top hats, but most of all my father enjoyed being both the owner and the driver of such a regal car. It appealed to his sense of the absurd, which suggested that people who could afford to be driven in a Rolls-Royce would never consider sitting behind the wheel and actually driving it themselves. James not only considered it, he relished it. He had a need to be a bit outlandish. My father was unabashedly pretentious and enjoyed being unabashedly outrageous.

As soon as the midnight-blue Rolls-Royce was delivered from the New York dealership, James insisted that Jennieame accept a ride in it. "Come on, Jenniemae, I'll take you home in the Rolls," he told her one evening after she had finished cleaning up.

"Oh no, we are not doin' some ridin' in that car. I will jus' go on and catch that old bus or you can take me in that comfortable wagon. I am not in any way ridin' down to my house in a big fancy car like that."

"Just this once. It will be fine," he insisted.

"I can't."

"Why not?" he asked.

" 'Cause I jus' can't."

"Oh, sure you can."

"Let me jus' get that bus, Mister James. I'll be fine," Jenniemae said, tired from the day's work.

"Please?" he pleaded.

"Oh Lord, you're just like the children."

"Just this once, then we can go back to the wagon," he said as he opened the passenger door to let her in as if he were the chauffeur.

The Rolls slowly headed down Connecticut Avenue with the two of them sitting in the front seat. James wore his typical three-piece suit and bow tie and Jenniemae was bundled in her warm black coat. It was winter, almost Christmastime—cold, clear, and brisk—with people walking along the streets carrying newly purchased gifts. As they drove through the crowded streets downtown, people turned to see who was in the shiny midnight-blue Rolls. At each red light pedestrians found themselves transfixed by what they saw: a white driver and a black passenger. James delighted in this shake-up of standards. Breaking rules, whether mathematical or social, was exciting for him. For Jenniemae, an event that drew attention to her was awkward and uncomfortable. When the Rolls approached South Carolina Avenue at Fourth Street—Jenniemae's neighborhood—many eyes watched the big car roll down the street. Immediately Jenniemae told James to stop.

"Don't you be leavin' me in front of my house in this car," she insisted.

"Why?" he asked, although he knew.

"Why? Why you askin' me why?"

"It will be fine."

"No it ain't. It ain't one bit of fine at all."

"You can't care what people say or think."

"No, honey," Jenniemae said, staring at him. "*You* don't have to care what people say or think, but I *do*. I have to be carin' 'cause that is jus' the way it is. So you jus' pull this big ole' hearse thing here along and let me off a far way away from my house."

"Hearse?"

"Yes indeed—it looks like a white man's hearse to me."

"This is how leaders of countries and movie stars travel, Jenniemae."

"Now, do I look like a movie star? Do I look like I will be leadin' a country anytime soon? Do I now, Mister James? Lord have mercy here!"

"Jenniemae . . ."

"Don't go Jenniemaein' me here. Jus' you stop this here thing up here aways," she insisted.

He agreed to let her out three blocks north of her house. "But I will watch you walk home," he said.

And so when Jenniemae got out of the Rolls, he slowly followed, inching along, keeping a half a block behind her as Jenniemae walked each street. Jenniemae kept turning around, trying to wave him away, but he would not leave. No doubt this caused a bigger scene in the neighborhood than if he'd just dropped Jenniemae off at her house.

By the time Jenniemae reached the stairs to her home, people were watching from their windows, wondering what was going on. And to make matters worse, as soon as Jenniemae began to climb the steps to her porch, he honked the horn twice as he drove off.

She shook her head and mumbled, "Lord have mercy, that man has no sense."

# CHAPTER TWENTY-TWO

*"No man is a stranger to trouble."*

One cold morning in December of 1956, while Jenniemae was doing the dishes, her telephone—the one in the back room—rang. Assuming it was someone asking about her morning number, she calmly turned the water off, dried her hands, and walked into her room. No sooner had she lifted the receiver off the telephone base than she could hear Lila Belle's screams. Jenniemae stopped breathing and her heart began to pound so fast she could feel its pulse through her skin. Even before she could put the receiver to her ear, Jenniemae's mind rushed through all the possible disasters that might be occurring to her Lila.

It turned out that Lila had been severely burned when Jenniemae's sister Cora accidentally knocked a pot of boiling water from the edge of the stove. Lila was now eighteen months old and Cora took care of her, along with her own two children, while Jenniemae was at work. Cora's husband, Raymond, worked days for the Sanitation Department and Cora worked nights for the U.S. Postal Service. There never was a question as to who would care for Lila—it was an unspoken understanding that when Cora was home with her own children, she would add Lila to the mix, and when Jenniemae returned home in the evenings, she would look after Cora's children.

It was the kind of accident that could happen in any kitchen. Lila had been sitting on the kitchen floor playing with a few wooden spoons when the pot just slipped out of Cora's hand. Before she could either catch it or snatch Lila away, the hot water spilled and Lila let out a terrifying scream. Cora picked her up and ran down the hallway to the telephone. With Lila crying hysterically in her arms, she dialed Jenniemae's number, and when Jenniemae picked up the receiver, all she could hear on the other end was her baby crying.

"Lord, what is it?" Jenniemae yelled into the telephone.

"Oh, honey, Lord, Lord . . . she's burned real bad. You got to come home fast and help. You got to come home right now."

"What happened?"

"The boiling water just spilled . . . it slipped . . . and it was an accident. Oh Lord ha' mercy I'm sorry . . . you got to hurry home."

"Lord, Lord have mercy. How bad is it? How bad?"

"Real bad. What should I do?"

"Oh Lord, baby girl."

"But what should I do?"

"Lord," Jenniemae kept repeating. "Did you run cold water over it?"

"It's worse than that. You got to get here now!" Cora screamed over Lila's cries.

"Oh Lord, how am I gonna get there fast enough? Where is she burned?"

"It's on her shoulder and . . . her arm."

"Run that cold water and I'll get there as soon as I can. You hear me now? Run it under the cold water." As frantic as Jenniemae felt—and she still could feel her heart pounding and her head aching—she knew that she had to stay focused. She had to think what to do next, how to get home as fast as possible, and how to best advise Cora until she got there. "I'm on my way, Cora. I'm on my way."

Jenniemae hung up the receiver and for a moment stood next to the telephone, paralyzed with fear. It was an awful feeling— her daughter was crying for help and she was not there. The best she could do was to stop thinking and just put herself in motion, place one foot in front of the other and act.

She hurried up the stairs to tell James that she had to leave.

"I got to go. Lila's hurt."

"What?"

"I'm on my way out now, Mister James," she said, turning to leave.

"Where to? Why?"

"Home. Lila's hurt."

"How hurt?"

"Burned and it's bad . . . Cora's got her."

"Cora?"

"My sister. I got to go."

"Oh . . . wait . . . I'll take you."

"No, no. I can do it on my own. I got to go now. I got no time. No time," she told him frantically.

"Let's go," he said, following her down the stairs and grabbing his overcoat on the way. "Get in the car. I'll take you."

As they sped down Connecticut Avenue, neither Jenniemae nor James said a word. Jenniemae looked straight ahead, willing the green lights to stay green or the red lights to turn green. She prayed that the other cars on the road would move out of the way so that they could get past. James concentrated on the road. As difficult as he could be, he was also extraordinarily caring and generous. And he was good during emergencies. In fact, the worse the situation, the calmer he seemed to get, which helped Jenniemae. Close to half an hour later they pulled up to the curb in front of Jenniemae's house. Before the car had come to a complete stop, she had opened the door.

"Wait," James said as he applied the brakes. For a large woman she could move very quickly when necessary, and this was one of those necessary times. She shot out of the car and barreled up the stairs to her house like an athlete. James watched her go. There wasn't much more he could do. His world and her world divided here in southeast D.C. She knew his house and his family and his world but only because she had to know it. The fact that they had formed a friendship—if that is what it could be called—was unusual and they both knew it. That friendship wasn't something either of them would ever discuss. Why discuss something that worked? If they could laugh about similar incidents, then so be it. If they felt empathy for each other, then so be that. And if they felt anxious over each other's problems, then that, too, was just what it was. Jenniemae certainly had more insight into the way James lived than he had into her world. He could listen to her daily sayings and enjoy her numbers game. He could try to help when she was confronted with difficult situations. He could offer more money, time off, even an ear to listen to her troubles. But when it came to entering into her world, he was stymied. He could drive her home, but he would never have asked to come into her house nor would she have ever considered inviting him. Their shared world ended at her front door.

Sitting in the station wagon in front of Jenniemae's house, James felt useless. He supposed that she expected him to leave, but he couldn't make himself do that. He decided he would wait in the car for a while. Perhaps Jenniemae would look outside after a few minutes and see him sitting there. Perhaps she would come out and tell him everything would be fine. Perhaps she would rush out and ask for his help. So he sat and watched the front door.

Nothing happened. The door didn't open and he couldn't see any movement through the windows. But he could hear the cries of a baby. After a few minutes he found himself standing uncomfortably at Jenniemae's front door. He could hear Jenniemae and her sister yelling back and forth. He could hear Lila crying. Knocking would be ridiculous, he thought, since they would never hear him, and even if they did, they wouldn't want to leave the baby in order to answer. So he pushed open the heavy wooden door, which opened onto a dark hallway of black and white linoleum tiles. He stood in the entryway for a few seconds waiting for his eyes to adjust to the darkness. He made his way slowly toward the crying and voices he could hear coming from a room at the end of the dark hallway. It was a small kitchen, no more than ten by twelve feet. A single light-bulb hung from a ceiling chain. James stopped at the doorway and saw that Jenniemae was bent over the sink, holding Lila's shoulder and arm under running water. The baby wailed and kicked.

That is how he described the scene when he told the story to our family later that night. We sat listening to every word as he tried to explain what had happened. That afternoon, while my brother and I were at school and Ruth was at work, he had entered into Jenniemae's secret-to-us world. No matter that Jenniemae was an important, integral part of our family, the fact was we would never have that role in her family. Jenniemae lived "in" our lives, she worked "in" our lives, she advised our lives, tended to and cared for our lives—but we were never going to do the same in her life. Not only would it have been unaccept-able—she would never have wanted us to interfere with matters of where or how she lived her life—we never would have even considered doing such a thing.

Ruth asked him, "Were you frightened?"

"By what?"

"By trying to help when you—well, maybe you weren't being asked to help," she said a little awkwardly.

"Well, truthfully, I was nervous about it, but then when I saw

Lila's arm and Jenniemae's face, I just did what anyone would have done. You would have done the same," he said, though he probably was not at all sure this was true.

James had entered Jenniemae's kitchen. Cora was standing beside the sink, tears running down her face. No one noticed him. For a moment he considered turning and walking back down the hallway to the car, but instead he said, "Can I help? Can I do anything?"

Jenniemae turned around, surprised to see him, but she had no time or patience to ask why he would take the liberty to enter her house.

"I just thought I would see if I could help," he said almost apologetically, realizing that she was somewhat taken aback.

Jenniemae's eyes looked blurred with fear. "It's bad," she said, somewhat out of breath. "Real bad." The boiling water had run from Lila's shoulder down onto her arm and much of the affected skin had already turned white.

"Maybe we should get her to a hospital. Maybe . . . right away," he said softly.

"Oh Lord."

"I think so, Jenniemae. I think it would be a good idea," he said, knowing her aversion to doctors.

"Lord."

"Come on now. Let's go," he prodded.

"Well . . . I suppose maybe so."

"How about I take you? In the car. Now."

Jenniemae wrapped Lila in a blanket, and with Cora she

followed James down the hallway and out to the car. "Where is the nearest hospital?" James asked.

"There's a hospital down about five blocks ... but it's not ... the Freedmen's Hospital," Jenniemae told him. Freedman's Hospital was the teaching hospital for Howard University College of Medicine and the place most black people would go if they could.

"We can't be going all the way over there now," Cora said. "We've got to go to the closest hospital down here."

"Yes, I know. Yes," Jenniemae agreed.

James remained silent on the subject. He felt he could not interfere in this decision. Obviously it would be easier for Jenniemae and for Lila if the doctors they were about to see were black doctors. James knew that. A few hospitals had been built specifically to treat the black population. There was Freedman's Hospital in Washington and Provident Hospital in Baltimore, Provident Hospital in Chicago and George W. Hubbard Hospital in Nashville. All of these hospitals had been established in the late 1800s to treat black people and to educate black doctors. Though by 1956 most "other" hospitals would also permit entry and treatment for a black person, it was also true that most black people felt extremely uncomfortable having white doctors and nurses examine them. James was well aware of this as he drove toward the hospital. Being Jewish, he did understand, for there had been numerous times when he'd experienced anti-Semitism, not to mention that he'd had relatives murdered in German concentration camps. He understood discrimination.

It was another thing James and Jenniemae had in common, and by no means was it a small thing.

Minutes later James pulled up to the emergency entrance of the closest hospital and let Cora and Jenniemae, who was carrying Lila, out of the car. "Can't park there!" a man shouted, and when James didn't respond, again he called out, "Can't park there!" But James got out and locked the doors. He had no intention of taking the time to move the car.

For a downtown hospital, the emergency room almost seemed too quiet to James. He had been in enough emergency rooms in his lifetime—having had five heart attacks, pneumonia, and other health emergencies from his youth on—to know that an empty emergency room was usually a sign of a bad hospital. But there was no time to search for another place. Even the white floor tiles looked worn and cracked. From the voices coming from behind closed curtains, it was clear that two patients were being treated. A third was sitting on a metal framed bed carefully cradling what might be a broken arm. Two nurses, both white, sat behind a long counter and looked up from their paperwork as Jenniemae appeared with a crying Lila in her arms. One rose as Jenniemae walked toward the desk. Cora stood beside her.

"What is going on here?" the nurse asked with clear irritation.

"It's my baby," Jenniemae replied.

"But what is going on?" the nurse snapped.

James came up and said, "We have a hurt baby. We need help."

The nurse looked curiously at James and then at Jenniemae and Lila. "And?"

"And what?" James said, obviously angry. "We need to see the doctor."

" 'We?' "

"We," he replied clearly.

"Fine. Let's get her to a bed." The nurse relented and led them to a corner bed.

It took close to an hour before a doctor appeared. James was furious but Jenniemae made it clear that he shouldn't cause any disturbance. "We need to jus' get her some medicine and then we can be goin' on our way, so settle down," she said a number of times as they waited.

"What happened here?" the doctor asked Jenniemae as he bent over to look at Lila's arm.

"Water spilled . . . boiling water that was in a pot spilled on her." Tears began to run down Jenniemae's face. She didn't want to cry in front of the doctor but couldn't help herself. Cora stood quietly in the corner, obviously feeling horrible about what had happened to Lila while under her care.

"We thought it might be a good idea to bring her here," James interjected. "It looks bad."

The doctor paid little attention to James and examined Lila's shoulder and arm. "Well, this isn't good. These are some serious burns here. She needs antibiotics."

"What?" Jenniemae asked.

"She has to be treated. This is serious. Antibiotics are what she needs, and she needs them now and intravenously."

"What does that mean?" she asked.

"It means that she has to stay here for a while."

"What kind of while?"

"A week, maybe more," the doctor said. "She needs fluids and has to have special bandages that are changed frequently."

"What? A week? A week here in the hospital?" Jenniemae cried out.

"Well, it takes at least a week. But we'll see how it goes," the doctor said.

"She can't stay no week in no hospital here."

"She has to."

"Oh God," James groaned, realizing this wasn't going to be easy.

"No. She can't," Jenniemae said.

"She'll be in good hands here," James tried.

"No she won't," Jenniemae said. "She has to come home."

"Jenniemae, she is better off here," James told her. "They can change the bandages and help her heal faster."

"No," Jenniemae said.

"Jenniemae. You'll be here with her all the time. You won't have to come to work. You can stay here with her. . . . She can be with her baby all the time, right?" he asked the doctor.

"Close to almost all the time," the doctor agreed.

"No," Jenniemae said.

"She will be better off here," the doctor said.

"Oh Lord. In a bed here? In a room here?"

"Yes, otherwise her burns could become badly infected. This is not about choice; it is about necessity," the doctor suggested.

"I don't take well to necessity."

"Well, this time I think you should," James offered.

"Do I have a choice?" she asked.

"You have a choice, but they say that necessity can even break iron, Jenniemae, and this is a necessity," James replied.

"All right, then. I'm not about to bend no iron."

# CHAPTER TWENTY-THREE

*"Most every man be good,*

*but not every man be good for everything."*

Jenniemae sat by Lila's hospital bed all day long the first days, and, curiously, the person who most often visited was Ruth.

Ruth came every day. When she arrived her arms were filled with gifts. She brought crayons and paper, dolls, stuffed animals, a beaded necklace. She brought a new soft pink-and-yellow blanket for Lila and two very pretty flower-print dresses with long sleeves to cover her bandages. Jenniemae, who was surprised by Missus Ruth's generous attendance, was also very flattered and pleased. She understood how busy Missus Ruth was—she was always working long hours—but when it came to acting from the heart, Missus Ruth never seemed to be comfortable.

Well dressed and in high heels to compensate for her five foot two inches, Ruth was always well made up. Appearance mattered to her. She enjoyed the stares and catcalls of men on the streets and she enjoyed using her looks to attract men she met socially. Dressing smartly helped compensate for her shyness.

And over the years, frequently called upon to host large dinner parties or social gatherings for people she hardly knew, she had worked hard not to appear shy or withdrawn. She made a point of being able to recall everyone's name and their children's names, how old their children were and where they were going to school—few would have suspected how truly uncomfortable she felt in these settings. By 1956, Ruth had become an extremely busy woman. She had received her Ph.D. in clinical psychology, was working at the National Institute of Mental Health in Bethesda, Maryland, and also had begun a private practice with a full schedule of patients. When not working, she wrote poetry, sculpted, and painted wonderful oils and watercolors. And by 1956 she was also a quite unhappy wife who had recently taken up with an attentive though not too demanding lover. Between her heavy work schedule, her art, and her new lover, Ruth had scant time to spend at home. Clearly this was one way in which she dealt with her miserable marriage and her loneliness. Caring for unhappy people outside the family was undoubtedly her best talent, which helped to explain why she was at Lila's bedside so often in the hospital.

Jenniemae wanted to ask Missus Ruth why she was so attentive and generous with Lila, who was not her own, but she knew better. It was strange how people could be—just strange.

One afternoon when Lila was napping, Ruth and Jenniemae found themselves sharing stories. One word led to another, and before they knew it, Jenniemae was telling Missus Ruth stories about her life in Alabama.

"I don't recall it all in entirety but we lived in a small place with a porch out front that we used to sit on," Jenniemae told her. "I recall that porch because we would spend nights out there when the air was too suffocating to catch a breath on the insides. There were nights that the swamp heat inside was worse than the swamp heat outside. We would be grabbin' pieces of anything around just to fan ourselves. We would take down the branches from the trees and use them as fans, and I recall that as well as most anything. I also recall that Mama always had a rule for us about those fans. Matter o' fact, there was a rule to fit every single breath of the day—a rule for gettin' up and a rule for washin' up, a rule for makin' the morning food and a rule for eatin' it, a rule for prayers and a rule for prayin', a rule for cleanin' and a rule for workin' the field. There were special Sunday rules and Monday rules. My mama was strict but she had a soft heart inside. A rule was a rule, a word was a word, and when she said a thing, we never questioned the reason why or how. Mama could get respect from us any ole time of the night or day. But when it came to our daddy, it was different. Mama said that when she first met our daddy, he was a good man who was hardworking, but then 'cause of the hardness of life down there and 'cause of all the liquor he drank to make the hardness seem soft, he grew into a man with a deaf ear, a blind eye, and a foul mouth."

Jenniemae looked out the window at the barren elm tree across the hospital parking lot and drifted to another place in her life, another time. Hissop, Alabama. Her mother, her drunken father, her older brothers and younger sisters, that old run-down one-room shack that had cracks in the walls and cracks in the floorboards and cracks in the roof where water dripped through during rainstorms. As a little girl Jenniemae had always figured that when there was a thunderstorm the lightning could cut a path right through the roof just like the water did and come right on in to the house. The water was one thing—it was a bother—but the lightning was another thing altogether. Jenniemae feared the lightning. She recalled that her father disappeared every night to go to some bar down the road and when he came home late at night he would be as drunk as the thunder and lightning combined. Jenniemae's mother would put up with it as well as any woman could, hardly letting out a scream when he shoved her against the wall and pushed her violently onto their old cot, ripping the clothes off her frail body, and then mounting her as if he were about to ride an animal. And her mama would lie there still as a dead nothing. Jennieame remembered the white flashes of lightning—the naked drunk man slapping her mother and her mother trying not to cry, not to even let one small sound out—and then it would be over and silent for a few hours, and when they awoke the next morning, their father would get up, pull on his pants and shirt, and walk out of the house as if nothing had ever happened. Even after he'd left the front yard, the entire house would still smell of his liquor and dead cigarettes. Jenniemae's mama would slowly rise from her bed, look at each of her children and say nothing, not one word. Jenniemae recalled how they all knew to be quieter than dead, and knew to sit and wait to be told when it was safe to speak or safe to move or safe to eat. Then their mama would put herself together, with swollen eyes and bruised lips, a scratch here and there, and she would pull a flow-ery print dress over her thin, worn body, and it would hide all the scars and scratches as if the night before had never happened—nor the night before that.

Ruth watched Jenniemae. She said, "You all right, Jenniemae?"

And Jenniemae replied, "Lila here doesn't have no daddy, and maybe that's a better thing in the long run, 'cause she doesn't have to see a good man being turned into a bad man."

"I understand," Ruth said.

"Do you?" Jenniemae asked.

"Yes, I do."

"What was your mama and daddy like, Missus Ruth?" Jenniemae asked.

Ruth hesitated for a minute. "Well, my mother, Belle, was a wonderful person," she began. "She was a beautiful Southern belle . . . and I really loved her."

Jenniemae said, "I bet she was and I bet you do."

"But she was unlucky in life and she had it hard. Maybe not hard in the same way your mother had it, but it was difficult. Hard times come in lots of different shapes and shades, don't they?"

Jenniemae nodded and said, "That they do, Missus Ruth. That they do."

"I was her only child," Ruth said. She paused, and then continued. "My father left us when I was two. I think he loved my mother at one time—but then maybe he didn't. Maybe he never loved her but felt he had to get married because that is what young men did in their twenties or thirties back then.

He married my mother after they had only known each other one month. There obviously wasn't much to their courtship—I know that—and I know that they met down in Shreveport, Louisiana, in 1910 when he was stationed on a naval ship outside New Orleans. The only story I ever heard about his being on any ship had to do with the building of the Panama Canal. I don't know but maybe his ship went down to Panama—though I couldn't say that for sure since the Canal didn't open until 1914. He never talked much about those days. My father was a quiet man—like a lot of Yankees from way north, you know?"

"Yes, I think I do know. People in the South—well, they like to talk a piece while people up farther north like to listen more than they like to talk." Jenniemae smiled.

"Yes, that's the truth. My father was from Waterville, Maine— a real northerner—and he grew up in a place that was about as far from Shreveport, Louisiana, as a person could get. If it hadn't been for the navy, they never would have met and then I never would have been born."

"Oh Lord, you can't think like that. The Lord has a plan and we jus' go with that plan," Jenniemae offered.

Ruth chuckled. "Maybe so. Maybe so. But it's any guess as to how my parents met. Shreveport isn't on the coast, but I suppose there must have been some occasion when he was off the ship and made his way there. Who knows if they met at a county fair or while just walking in the park or at some formal event. She was beautiful, so it wouldn't have been difficult for him to notice her in a crowd. My mother never said what happened, and neither did he. To me that was always one obvious sign that they both would rather have forgotten that meeting and wished it had never occurred than have to recall it and relate it to their daughter, who was an accident of nature, anyway."

"Now, that's no way to talk, Missus Ruth, no way." Jenniemae shook her head.

"But it's the truth. Anyway, they married and moved to New York City, which she always hated. She didn't like the people and she didn't like the noise. She always said she would move back to Shreveport one day. But my father had work in the city, so she didn't have much say in the matter. He worked as an accounting clerk for a few years and then I was born in 1914. He stayed around for two more years until he couldn't stand it any longer. One morning he left for work and didn't return. Just like that. He wrote my mother a letter a few weeks later when he was in Florida and said he just couldn't see spending his life being tied down to one place, one woman, one family. It just didn't suit him and he had a passion for gambling that was greater than any passion he had for my mother. He didn't *say* he loved gambling more than he loved her, but that's what I grew up knowing, because it was true. He traveled up and down the East Coast playing the horses and dogs, and he'd appear at our apartment every few years just as if nothing had ever happened. He wouldn't stay for longer than forty-five minutes, because he always said he had to be somewhere else. I knew he wasn't there to see my mother and that he just wanted to see what kind of young girl I was growing up to be. I was always thrilled to see him, but my mother fumed when he came and watched the clock until he left again. So I saw my father once every two or three years and between times I wrote him letters that I never sent because there were no addresses to send them to. Sometimes I dreamed about taking trips with him and I drew pictures of him that I kept in my secret diary. I imagined him into a wonderful person that he never really was.

"His name was Ernest. Isn't it funny that a name should mean so little and so much at the same time? *Ernest* means sincere and honest. Well, I cannot say he was honest, but I think he was sincere with me, usually. He wasn't a loyal man, but he did seem to love me. And if it hadn't been for all the things that went with having a child—such as having an unhappy wife he had to listen to every evening or having to go to an office and settle for the boredom of day-to-day work—I think he would have been delighted to have a daughter or a son. Though maybe not. Maybe that is wishful thinking on my part. He wasn't a bad person; he just couldn't figure a good way out of a bad marriage, so he decided to just up and walk out. Divorce wasn't something too many people did then, and I'm fairly certain that he didn't feel it would be a good option. And maybe for once he was trying to consider my mother's feelings by not asking for a divorce. He knew that she would have been devastated to have to tell her family or friends that she and her husband were divorcing. It was easier to just pretend he was traveling somewhere for work and that one day he would return. It was easier for them to live like that, in the thick of a lie, than it would have been to tell the truth. My mother was happier without him and he was happier without her. Even when my mother fell ill and he heard about it through relatives, he didn't come to take care of her—or me. I think he was frightened by the thought of having to care for either of us since he had no training for it."

Jenniemae couldn't help but be struck by how some of the things Missus Ruth was telling her about her parents were true in Missus Ruth's own marriage. Even though Mister James and Missus Ruth lived under the same roof, they lived separately and they surely didn't live with a lot of truth. Jenniemae would never have opened up this can of worms, though. Instead she simply asked, "Why was your mama sick?"

"She got breast cancer."

"Oh Lord, I am sorry to hear that," Jenniemae said sincerely.

"Yes, it was horrible. And I was just a child. It was summertime when she became seriously ill, and since she didn't want to have me around when she died, I was sent off to camp. A telegram was sent to the camp on the day my mother died." She paused. "I was escorted home by a counselor for the funeral. My father never showed, and since there was nowhere for me to live, I was handed over to a great-uncle and -aunt who lived in the city. They didn't really want to take care of me. They were childless and had no desire to care for me or any child, for that matter. The only reason they took me in was because I had a small inheritance, which they promptly stole from me. All of it. Every single penny. As soon as I was old enough to run away, I did."

"You ran away from your home, Missus Ruth?"

"It never was a place to call home. It was my uncle's house, not my home. I did run away. I was fifteen, and one day I decided

I couldn't live with them any longer. So I packed my few belongings in a satchel and ran off to live with my friend Shirley Gross, who lived on Riverside Drive."

"Did they come and find you?" Jenniemae asked.

"They never once looked for me."

"Lord have mercy."

"But I have a good life now, don't I?" Ruth asked.

"Sure you do, Missus Ruth. Sure you do. You have a plenty good family now. You got two beautiful children and a fine husband and a nice house," she said, trying to convince Missus Ruth of something that needed convincing.

"I do have two beautiful children. One fine husband, well . . ." She smiled; both of them knew that it would be hard to call James a "fine husband." He may have been many things but a fine husband wasn't one of them. It had occurred to Ruth more than once that she may have subconsciously looked for a man who wouldn't be faithful or loyal—like her own father. She had found a man who had been married three times before, which was clearly not a great track record for loyalty, and even when they were already engaged, he had gone off to be with another woman. With James, Ruth knew that she had a bright, clever, attractive man who would probably not be loyal, whether or not they married or had children.

A nurse walked in to change Lila's bandages and this ended the conversation, which was probably just as well. Both Jenniemae and Ruth sat for a while considering all that had been shared. Neither regretted the conversation, but neither wanted to continue it.

"It's getting late. I really should head home," Ruth said as she stood to leave.

"Thank you for coming to visit. And thank you very much for the gifts, Missus Ruth. Lila loves it when you show up in that doorway. You are too nice."

"Thank *you*, Jenniemae," Ruth said, and left.

Never again did they talk as they did that afternoon, but the conversation didn't disappear. Once the words were said, they were not going to be forgotten even if they would never again be mentioned. Both Missus Ruth and Jenniemae had given a little bit of themselves to the other and both respected that they had done so.

# CHAPTER TWENTY-FOUR

*"A howling dog knows what he sees."*

Lila was unhappy in the hospital. The noises frightened her. The lights bothered her. The nurses were less than friendly and the doctors gave her as little time as possible. She had been put in a small room at the end of the corridor that looked as if it had been recently converted from a storage closet. Jenniemae never would have complained. It wasn't her style to complain, and she assumed it would probably only make things worse. But everything about the hospital was white: The doctors were white, the nurses were white, the walls were white, the bedding was white—being a black overweight woman with a black baby in a white hospital was way out of her comfort range.

There were other black children in the hospital—births, injuries, illnesses, and deaths—but most of them came, got treated, and left. Negroes didn't usually stay long at this hospital or any other hospital, for that matter. Most couldn't afford to pay for the medical care, and moreover, they didn't trust the white doctors. So after only eight days, Jenniemae decided enough was enough. She could give her daughter better care at home. She packed up Lila's belongings, bundled her up in the blanket Missus Ruth had brought, and walked out the door, past the nurses' station, and onto the elevator. No one said a word, although they knew the baby was supposed to be in the hospital longer.

Jenniemae cared for Lila at home, applying to the burns a plant lotion she had purchased from a healer who lived down the block. The burns healed and Lila's arm became stronger, though it would never be as strong or look the same as her right arm. There would always be scars. But as Jenniemae said, that would be the least of this child's worries, and who knew but that maybe an accident like this might make her a stronger woman later in her life.

"You got to stand soaked to the bone in a rainstorm and fill up your buckets with all the water heaven has given up," Jenniemae said. "Then when the sun comes out, you will have your savings and never find yourself thirsty. That's how it is."

# CHAPTER TWENTY-FIVE

*"If you do something secret in the dark,*

*then you can't be surprised when the sun comes up."*

Nineteen fifty-nine was the year that Fidel Castro seized power in Cuba and Charles de Gaulle became president of the Fifth Republic of France. It was also the year that the Soviets launched a "cosmic rocket" embossed with a hammer-and-sickle emblem that flew past the moon to orbit the sun. And it was the year that strontium 90, a radioactive isotope of the element strontium, was reportedly found in high levels in the United States. Strontium 90, a silver-gray metal, was the product of atomic explosions that widely dispersed the metal into the atmosphere. Ultimately, the metal dust fell to the ground. In 1959 it was discovered that strontium 90 had settled onto the farmlands where cows grazed. Now this extremely dangerous radioactive toxin was in the milk that millions of children drank every day. The press reported that exposure to strontium 90 could be lethal; that people exposed to it could receive serious radiation injuries such as shortness of breath with pulmonary crepitus, or could fall into a coma or even die. Almost everyone in the country heard the reports about strontium 90, and almost everyone was frightened by what they heard. In our house our father announced one evening that we would no longer be drinking or eating dairy products. No milk, cottage cheese, or cheese. We agreed with him, but Jenniemae was skeptical. It took days to convince her.

"You want me to throw out all this good milk?"

"It might have poisonous particles in it."

"Who says?"

"Scientific studies."

"Which means nothin'."

"Jenniemae, it's an unnecessary risk. Don't use dairy products and you shouldn't give them to Lila."

"First they tell us they are protectin' us all, and then they tell us they're poisonin' us. Which is it?"

"Both. And maybe neither."

"That's the truth. Both and neither. That is the truth."

"But take my word, it's not worth the risk. It's just milk and cheese."

"All right, then," she said, and dairy products were removed from our house.

In 1959 the country was growing disillusioned by what had been billed as great advances in science that would make all Americans better, healthier, and stronger, and let them live longer. People who once believed their country had their best interests at heart began to worry that perhaps their country's scientific advances might be killing them. In addition to the strontium 90 scare, they wondered why the government was constantly testing H-bombs. Was there going to be another war? Was World War

III about to happen? Reports began appearing in the news that the communist North Vietnamese were moving into Laos and that this posed a potential threat to the United States. Most Americans had little idea where North Vietnam even was and were not clear as to why the movements of the North Vietnamese threatened us. Some knew there was something called the "foreign policy domino theory," but connecting the dots of that theory to what was going on in some Asian country they had never heard of before was a hard argument to make. And while some had grown weary of hearing about the potential threats to democracy because of the spread of communism, it was also true in 1959 that most Americans believed the Soviet Union had become a far more powerful and potentially dangerous country than before. Many American families feared that the USSR would drop atomic bombs on the United States. In fact, quite a number of families dug up their backyards and installed fallout shelters, believing that somehow they would be safe after "the bomb" exploded, and that somehow entire families could live in these shelters for some undetermined amount of time, then emerge one day to—who knew what?

To add to these anxieties, another conflict had been brewing and intensifying throughout the 1950s. By 1959, African-American men and women across the nation were tired of being treated like third-class citizens and they were beginning to speak out. The integration of public schools mandated by *Brown v. Board of Education* in 1954 had been progressing slowly and with much resistance, particularly in the South. In September of 1957, Little Rock, Arkansas, governor Orville Faubus had ordered 270 National Guard troops to prevent nine black students from entering Central High School. The students returned home but anger was mounting. There were rumors of freedom marchers possibly disrupting the peace, and of angry mobs entering the city. Fearing that violence might erupt, President Eisenhower ordered federal troops into Little Rock. Command posts and tents were set up and finally, with tensions high, the black students were escorted into Central High, while Faubus declared that the troops were "bludgeoning innocent bystanders." The civil rights movement was gaining momentum and attention.

James's involvement in the civil rights movement was one of honest empathy. He had always been an advocate for civil rights but he wasn't one to participate in marches or protests. His passion, his knowledge, and his focus were on the threat of another war. He devoted most of his energies and much of his work now to fighting for world peace and arguing against the further development and proliferation of nuclear weapons alongside the possible use of atomic bombs. He was engaged in bitter battles against those who believed that nuclear warfare was at all reasonable.

In a letter to *The Washington Post* he wrote:

> It is best not to qualify what cannot be qualified. The attempt ends in absurdities. That the sun rises in the east, that yesterday cannot return, that man is mortal, are statements admitting of no exceptions. That a war of nuclear weapons is lunatic is in the same case. It is an uncontingent truth, beyond niggling or casuistry. One hears in our day a good

deal about the dignity of the individual. This is often coupled with the suggestion that while emblems and territory and treasure are not at our stage of civilization a justifiable casus belli, the dignity of the individual is worth fighting for. I cherish my individuality, and I respect the individuality of others. I know that many men are not free. But it does not occur to me that I can protect my dignity, and maintain or achieve that of others, by dropping atom bombs.... It is difficult to believe that when men are dead dignity will endure. It will vanish when they vanish.

Where are we going and what is the aim of responsible men? For the moment we must accept the bitter fact that the problem of disarmament offers no solution, that there is no ear in the world, as Einstein once remarked to me, for reasonable proposals. That is a hard fact, but we must learn to live with it until we can surmount it. Meanwhile we must deny ourselves the consolation of thinking that if the worse comes to worst we can retaliate by exterminating mankind. Such dreams we may leave to the malign, the demented and the irresponsible.*

---

*James R. Newman, "The Awful Deterrent" first appeared in *The Washington Post* and was then collected in *The Rule of Folly* (New York: Simon & Schuster, 1962), p. 50.

But this was not the only issue on James's plate that year.

In the spring of 1959, James had taken on a new lover named Katariina. Katariina was from Estonia, spoke very little English, was six feet four inches tall, had long, wavy, bleached orange-blond hair and blue eyes. James hired her to be his new secretary when his former secretary, Rachel, jumped off the Calvert Street Bridge in D.C. Rachel had been instantly killed when she hit the Rock Creek Parkway 150 feet below. She had been an efficient, bright, though somewhat homely single woman in her mid-forties who lived with another woman. We heard rumors that the roommates were "involved," they were lovers, and that Rachel's mother had discovered her daughter's dark and embarrassing secret, and that this "outing" then caused Rachel to become deeply despondent, which ultimately led to her decision to take her own life by climbing over the guard rails of the Calvert Street Bridge and jumping. Though I wanted to know every single detail of why my father's secretary would have made such a decision and what brought her to actually do it—perhaps I wanted to better understand the limits to which depression could bring a person—my mother said there was no reason to open the wounds of Rachel's personal story, given the tragic ending to her life, and it shouldn't be discussed. And though the words *lesbian* or *lovers* were never mentioned in our house, it certainly helped to explain why James hadn't had an affair with Rachel and why Ruth liked her so much.

In any event, weeks after Rachel's funeral, James interviewed seven or eight women to replace her, all of whom were either, according to him, illiterate, frumpy, or boring. However, when an eighteen-year-old girl who spoke very little English appeared at the front door, responding to his advertisement in the newspaper for a secretary, it didn't take long before James hired her—forty-five minutes at most. Within a month they were lovers.

"The darkness and the light are not alike and not s'posed to be alike," Jenniemae told me one afternoon. "People have got to know the difference 'tween the two since each time is meant for its own. I can tell you that any woman that slips between the sheets during both the dark and the light, without having a care 'bout the difference between them, is a no-good woman. Work is to be work and another thing is to be another thing." Jenniemae was upset about James's new girlfriend, who clearly was slipping between his sheets during the daytime—work time— and she didn't like any part of it going on in the house. It wasn't just that James had a new woman, since Jenniemae had become somewhat used to his women—it was that this woman, if she could be called a woman at eighteen, was "a leggy whore," according to Jenniemae. Jenniemae had no patience for Katariina. It didn't help that she spoke a strange, broken kind of English. Jenniemae believed that Katariina was no good and that she was using Mister James for his money and that she was exploiting his good will.

As for Katariina—she feared Jenniemae. Katariina was not stupid, no matter what Jenniemae might have thought, nor did she lack insight. She was well aware that Jenniemae didn't like her and wanted her to leave, and she was well aware that James had a close relationship with Jenniemae. Rather than try to develop any sort of friendship with Jenniemae by discussing the weather or the furnishings, or anything for that matter, Katariina chose to remain quiet and avoid Jenniemae whenever possible—which also suited Jenniemae just fine.

No matter what Katariina did or didn't do on any given day, Jenniemae's opinion of the girl remained constant: "There are some days I just stand and watch what goes on around this here house, jus' like a sparrow on the treetop lookin' down. I am jus' waitin' to see what is happenin' one minute and then waitin' to see what is going to happen the next, and all the while I know I am not likin' it. It's not a thing for me to judge, but I can't help it some days, because this here house is over-filled with make-believe. So much make-believin' that when I leave here at night I have a hard time being able to tell the color blue from red and yellow from pink. But I can tell you one thing for a fact, and that is that this foreign girl, she is the color of evil. She is an ugly, lyin' foreign girl with the color of evil under her skin."

Jenniemae didn't like Katariina's long, skinny legs, she didn't like her bleached blond "bottle hair," she didn't like her short skirts and tight blouses, she didn't like her bright red lipstick, and she surely didn't like her strange accent. And though I would never have admitted it in front of Jenniemae, I "sort of" liked Katariina. I did. I was used to having my father's girl-friends around, but before now they'd always been "older" women with whom I had nothing in common. With Katariina it was different—we were close in age, only four years between us. We could talk about music—we both mourned the plane crash that took the lives of Buddy Holly, Ritchie Valens, and the Big

Bopper. We both wore similar clothes and had close to the same color hair—though mine wasn't bleached blond. We never became good friends—that might have been awkward for both of us—but we were friendly. And most important, Katariina ingratiated herself with me when one day she secretly lent me her worn and partly torn copy of *Peyton Place* by Grace Metalious. Though I had heard rumors in school about this racy book, I had never seen it. Katariina confided that she had a copy and would lend it to me if I didn't tell anyone, so as soon as it was in my hands, I took it to my room, closed the doors, and pored over every wonderful, illicit page about sex, lust, abortion, incest, and murder. I probably read *Peyton Place* five times before returning it to her. One would have thought I would have been fairly savvy about sex, given what went on in my home, but that wasn't the case at all. I was extraordinarily naive and stunningly ignorant about anything sexual. In a house where sex was a constant source of turmoil and emotional angst in my parents' lives, I remained innocent and uninformed and in complete denial. To suggest that I wore thick blinders and well-made earplugs would be an understatement. For me, sex—whatever it was—was something that happened elsewhere or between the pages of books like *Peyton Place*. And since sex was not a topic ever discussed between my mother and me, or my father and me, it was easy for me to remain in denial. Both my parents avoided the topic and I never would have asked—and I surely didn't want to know if it had anything to do with them. In 1959 sex wasn't discussed in the classroom, and I don't recall talking about it with girlfriends. I don't know what I thought about sex—if I thought about it often or even at all—but I do know that Katariina's gift created a bond between us.

Katariina was openly my father's lover, clearly Jenniemae's nemesis, and quietly an uncommon sort of friend to me—all of which made this a different relationship from his other "women friends" to whom we had all become accustomed. While my father's other women friends were never exactly kept secret, their relationship with him was never mentioned, nor articulated, and in this way they were not given complete validity. Yet no matter how clandestine these affairs were, or how much credence they were or were not given, the women were very much a part of our lives. However, when Katariina arrived, these rules changed.

There never was any pretense of Katariina's being anything but James's girlfriend. James didn't pretend she was anything else and neither did Ruth. The words *lover* or *girlfriend* were never used, but they didn't have to be. Katariina did not sneak into James's room late at night, she simply joined him there. When she moved into the house months later, she was given a separate room, but slept with James in his room while Ruth stayed in her own room. When James took business trips to New York, Katariina joined him. The two of them stayed at the Stanhope Hotel on Fifth and Eighty-first and we all knew it. It was where they were if anyone needed to get in touch. Frequently Katariina and James dined out at D.C. restaurants without Ruth and, almost more peculiarly, on other occasions they all dined out together. Before Katariina, James had girlfriends who sometimes lived with us and sometimes didn't, but he always kept up the slight pretense that the two weren't really lovers. This time, however, everything was on the up-and-up. Maybe it had something to do with the tense political cloud that hung over the country in 1959 or maybe it had to do with Ruth and James's marriage eroding. Maybe it had to do with James grasping for a youth he never had. Maybe it had to do with a fatigue connected with keeping things secret—but I seriously doubt that that was the case.

Ruth accepted this relationship—this one going on in her house, in the bedroom next to her own—with a strange relief. She didn't seem angry or frustrated or disappointed. Ruth not only accepted the affair between this young Estonian girl and her husband, she condoned it. In fact, Ruth and Katariina became close friends and confidantes. They played Scrabble together in the evenings. They discussed relationships, dreams, education, travel, women, fashions, hairstyles. They went to lunch together. Ruth advised Katariina on how to move forward with her life, with this relationship (the one with Ruth's own husband), and she encouraged Katariina (her husband's lover) to go on to college, even promising that she would help pay for Katariina's education. They laughed together and cried together and talked for hours on end about absolutely everything. And while I am certain that my mother was not as complacent about this affair as she seemed to be, it was also true that she probably did feel a sense of relief with Katariina around since—unbeknownst to anyone in the family—she, too, had fallen in love. She had more or less given up on fighting for her husband—not completely, just more or less. She didn't want to leave him—at least not yet—but she didn't really want to have him, either. She had been hurt and humiliated for so many years with one woman or another that she had become somewhat resigned to the pattern, and now after years of feeling this way, she stepped out on her own and somewhat defiantly had her own relationship on the side. I am sure this offered her a bit of self-confidence—something she rarely got from her husband—but it also allowed her a sense of retribution and self-satisfaction.

The more peculiar this setup with Katariina and James became, the more it infuriated Jenniemae. She was not going to have any part of it.

"That girl has got to go. It is bad luck if a blue jay flies into your house. You know that, honey?" she asked me one day.

"No, I didn't know that."

I wasn't bothered by this relationship or the ones that had come before Katariina—it was just the way things had always been. I didn't see anything strange about it—not really.

"And it is another bad luck when a wasp's nest falls off a rooftop. You understand me?"

"No, not really," I admitted again.

"Well, then, I am goin' to 'splain it to you 'cause it needs 'splainin' to. I am talkin' about the evil eye of a lie. You listen to me, honey."

"Okay." I *was* listening, but Jenniemae often liked to remind me to listen even when it wasn't necessary.

Jenniemae explained: "One lie will make a man squint his eyes. You've seen it. It happens. And then he goes on with the squintin' and he tells a second lie. And that second lie makes him squint even harder. Then here comes the third lie. Then the fourth, and soon enough the squintin' man has gone all blind by his lies."

"And?"

"And nothing . . . and this is what I am sayin'. This here foreign girl is makin' your daddy a blind man. And a blind man doesn't pay attention to his own house. That girl ain't nothing but a lyin' whore pretendin' to be elsewise. You understand me? Do you? What I'm tellin' you is that things happen when you can't see clear . . . things happen. While you are busy keepin' an eye out for the wasp nest fallin' down from the roof, another thing can happen and that thing might be bad. And likewise, while you are busy keepin' an eye out for that blue jay that might just be flyin' into your house, there just might be something else going on."

"And?"

"And the point is that while a person is payin' close attention to one thing . . . and that one thing is filled with all kinds of dishonesties . . . well, then, that person is goin' to lose focus on a whole lot of other things. And it is all those other things that you should be attendin' to. You understand?"

"Maybe. I think so."

"Point is that you can never be too careful about lies and bad luck walkin' straight in the front door while you're keepin' guard on the back door. That is what I mean. That is jus' what I mean."

"Oh. I suppose I understand."

I thought about what Jenniemae was saying and there was, of course, lots of truth in it. But I wasn't certain what the danger was at either the front or the back door. Was it the lovers? Or was it this particular lover? Or was it the danger of the strontium 90 or the spread of communism or the fallout shelters?

In the spring of 1959 I was fourteen years old. Besides having tried to completely distance myself from anything sexual, I had also tried to detach myself from most emotions and any possible conflicts. And in both instances I had been unwittingly unsuccessful. No matter how innocent I may have seemed, I was not entirely so. No matter how naive I was, I was also not entirely oblivious. I was disengaged and perhaps I had been too gullible in believing in the power and possibilities of pretending and keeping secrets. Perhaps I had believed too definitively that not admitting a thing existed might magically transform it into not existing. No matter what it was that I had grown up trying to do—I was not succeeding. I was a mess! I had, for the most part, given up eating anything beyond two apples a day, had lost a considerable amount of weight, and had begun to pull my hair out. In fact, I had pulled so much hair out that I had created two very large bald spots on the back of my head. And though I tried to hide the spots, attempting to brush hair over the area, my father noticed it one afternoon and was horrified. Thinking that I had contracted some disease, he took me to a dermatologist. I remember that appointment—the dermatologist examined me and asked that I sit in the waiting room while he talked to my father. After waiting for a painful twenty minutes, my father emerged from the dermatologist's office, smiled at me, and suggested we leave. Not a word was said. He took my hand in his. We rode the elevator to the parking garage, got into the car, and drove downtown to a store called Garfinkel, where he bought me a wonderfully soft, beige stuffed animal dog (which I named Farfel and still have to this day) and a gold bracelet (which I was forced to sell in a pawnshop when I was thirty-five). He gave me the dog, clasped the bracelet around my right wrist, and hugged me very hard. Not a word was ever said about my pulling my hair out, and though I loved my gifts, I was more thankful for his silence than anything else. I knew he knew and I knew he wouldn't make me discuss it with him.

Tension was everywhere and the things that were entering our house to cause that tension seemed inevitable and uncontrollable for me. Checking on the back door seemed as foolish as checking on the front door, but I understood what Jenniemae was trying to tell me. Bad luck was not a good thing to live with, and it might be invading our home.

Jenniemae didn't let up in advising me about the ill will that lies beget. "Lies are the cause of bad luck livin' right inside your own house. Lies cook up their own brew of bad luck sure as I am standin' here today and talkin' to you. And that is what is happenin' here, right now. That foreign girl is nothin' but lies bringin' in bad luck and she has to go. She is no good. And no good comes from no good."

"Okay."

"But that's not up to you. I'm just tellin' you about it."

"Okay," I repeated, knowing there was nothing I could do about my father's girlfriend or my mother's relationship with that girlfriend or any of it.

"I know you got your troubles here, honey. I can see that before my eyes and it worries me enough to be sick, but I am tellin' you this here girl is one more worry you don't need. You can't be frettin' about the milk and the wars that might happen and might never happen . . . can't be your worry at your age. But what is in your own home here, it is worth fightin' for, so I am goin' to bat here for you . . . and for me and for all of us. Because I know. Just because."

There wasn't anything I could do to convince her otherwise. I knew Jenniemae intended to do something, since once she had a notion to go after a thing, there was little that was going to stop her.

Soon after this conversation Jenniemae confronted James. "That girl has to go. You have to open that front door and show her the way out."

"Jenniemae, Katariina's a nice girl. She works hard and is trying to learn the language and make something of herself."

"Don't use her name in front of me. It is bad fortune." She shook her head. "And don't try me with that foolishness about her learnin' this or that thing. I'm no fool, Mister James."

"I realize that."

"Don't even try me. This is a bad-luck girl. No good is comin' from her, no good luck."

"Don't be ridiculous," he argued.

"I am not being anything but right. Lord have mercy, but you are under her spell. She is one bad-luck girl."

"She's trying to make something of herself."

"No she ain't, Mister James. No she ain't at all. She's tryin' to make a fool of you and this family. And she's doin' a good job of it. That girl knows where to put her head at night 'cause that's the same place she gets taken care of."

"It's not like that at all, Jenniemae," he said.

"Oh, Lord have mercy on me. You know it is exactly like that. You know it is so. And I don't take to it one bit."

"What would you have me say to her?"

"Say to her? Say to her nothin'. Give to her nothin'. Be to her nothin'."

"Are you suggesting I tell her to leave?"

"You know I am, Mister James. and you know that it's not good that she is here in front of the children and all."

"What do you mean?"

"Mister James, you got one son who is almost a man now and a daughter who is but a growin' girl. And now you got a girl hangin' on you who is . . . Lord have mercy, I don't need to be explainin' this to you, because you know it is true and you jus' don' want to hear it. Man isn't gonna hear what he don't want to hear, but I am not gonna sit by and say it is jus' fine and all right by me. 'Cause it isn't. That foreign girl ain't nothin' but badness in this here family."

"I can't kick her out," he said meekly.

"You can . . . but you won't. And Mister James, you look at

yo'self. You dressin' up like you was some twenty-year-old man tryin' to impress some whore."

"She's not a whore."

"To me she is. My way of thinkin' says she is nothin' but that."

"I can't just kick her out."

"Lord, Lord have mercy. She's gonna bring around a slew of barking dogs. And things are gonna get ugly after the dogs arrive."

"What is that supposed to mean?"

"Just what I say."

"Which is what?"

"Mister James, you mark what I am tellin' you. If you don't look straight in the eye of what is happenin' right here in your own house, then somethin' dark will come about. It jus' will happen."

"That's crazy."

"No, sir. It ain't crazy one bit."

"Jenniemae, I know what you're saying but I don't believe that luck comes into a house on the back of someone else. And I don't believe in luck, anyway—on a person's back or under a rock or behind a worm."

"Well, then, don't call it luck. Call it what is due a person when that person does a thing or two. Call it your own fate that you brewed up. If a man causes a thing to happen, then it ain't luck when it does happen—it is jus' your own brewed-up fate."

"True. I agree with that, but I don't agree that Katariina being here is my own brewed-up fate."

"Well, I hope I am wrong, then."

# CHAPTER TWENTY-SIX

*"The Lord, He makes*

*the skies to boil like a pot and*

*the land below to bear His heavy burden."*

Four months after this conversation—according to Jenniemae's calendar, Lila was four years, four months, and eleven days old—The Storm hit. Whether it had to do with that brewed-up fate Jenniemae had predicted would be anyone's guess. She was certain that it did. The newspaper, however, made no mention of Katariina's influence on weather patterns. However, there was information about a cold front and a high and a low coming together all at the same place and the same time. The weather forecasters had missed predicting the possible intensity of this storm, they explained days later, because of the unlikelihood that the cold front coming in after the previous heat wave, and the northern high-pressure system which collided with an eastern low-pressure system (or something like that), would all come together the way they did. The long and short of it was that the weather forecasters did not predict this "weather event," and had the wind gusts reached ninety-five miles per hour instead of the recorded ninety-one, it would have had to have been classified as a hurricane (there were a few unsubstantiated reports that people had clocked gusts at 110 miles per hour). No matter the miscalculations of the meteorologists and no matter the velocity of the wind, the people who lived in Washington, D.C., and the surrounding Virginia and Maryland suburbs knew damned well that this unnamed storm deserved to be called something more than just a "weather event," particularly given the damage it caused.

If the meteorologists had consulted Jenniemae on what was likely to happen, however, they would have been far more accurate. Not only had Jenniemae suggested four months earlier that some unsettled occurrence was likely, but two days before the storm hit, she had predicted it even more precisely. "Devil is gonna march right through this town real soon," she told me as she was peeling potatoes. "I can feel it all over. I can feel it under my skin. That's what is goin' to happen, you mark my words. You just wait and see."

"Why?" I asked, watching the red skins of the red potatoes fall into the bowl. She would always place the skins into a separate dish from the potatoes she was about to boil. Rarely was anything just tossed into the garbage if it could possibly be used. Even if my mother didn't want her to save the skins from the red potatoes or the peelings from carrots or the fat from the side of beef or the juice leftovers after browning the chicken—Jenniemae saved it. If she didn't use it in a dish that she prepared for our family, she would take it home at night in a bag for hers. "No sense of puttin' out to waste what some folks need. Don't matter what kind of food it is, 'cause an empty stomach makes a good cook out of any person" was a thing she frequently said.

"Are you askin' me why the devil is marchin' in?" she said.

"Yes, why is the devil coming?" I asked again.

"Because he is. Because of the black cat that is draggin' in the bad luck."

"What black cat?" I still didn't get it.

"That girl. Black cat of a girl. That's why."

"That's crazy, Jenniemae," I told her, knowing who she was talking about. "Nothing is going to happen like that," I said, though I wasn't positive. Often Jenniemae seemed to have some sense of what might happen even when it seemed like the most absurd possibility. There are some people—like Jenniemae— who you don't think you should believe when they tell you something far-fetched, but then you also don't think you *shouldn't* believe them either, because . . . just because you never know.

And, sure enough, forty-eight hours after this conversation, the storm hit. For people rising to go to work or children getting ready to go to school or truckers making deliveries or newspaper boys throwing the morning paper on front steps, there seemed to be nothing particularly unusual about that morning. Before the storm rolled in, the first light in the morning sky appeared, displaying long bands of deep red, purple, and yellow lines. An hour later, after the sun had risen, the sky had turned steel gray and was streaked with thin white clouds. It seemed as if this day would just be another warm, routine East Coast morning, with autumn-gray skies and hardly a breeze blowing. In fact, it was so calm that people left their homes wearing short-sleeved shirts and summer dresses. But if a person had taken the time, he or she would have noticed that there were no birds chirping in the trees or flying from telephone wire to telephone wire. In fact, there didn't seem to be any birds anywhere. An exodus of birds had taken place, mostly unnoticed. And if anyone had taken the time to search, they would have discovered that the birds had sheltered in the tall weeds and grasses of the inland marshes of the Chesapeake and Potomac Rivers. The birds knew what was about to happen. And if anyone had taken the time, they also would have noticed that the small ground animals, like the chipmunks and the gray squirrels, had disappeared, burrowing deep inside ground tunnels for safety. They, too, knew what was on the horizon. And as well, the horses in the pastures out on River Road, on the fancy horse farms with wooden split-rail fences, knew. The horses all turned their heads to face northward. And dogs sensed the coming storm—they paced and circled before finding sheltered areas where they could lie down.

This quiet was anything but quieting for the animals.

When a slight breeze drifted in from the south around mid-morning, the people walking down Wisconsin Avenue in Georgetown thought nothing of it and went about their business, as did the visitors to the Lincoln Memorial and the Washington Monument and those standing in line on Pennsylvania Avenue to tour the White House. Few gave it a moment's notice. A soft, warm breeze around mid-morning felt good amidst the usual humidity of D.C.

But not long after that breeze set in, the sky turned from

light gray to a deep, thick, steely gray and the winds began to pick up. What had been streaked clouds in the morning sky now were thick, dark cumulus clouds. Soon raindrops began to fall. Picnic table umbrellas that had been left out on patios and porches bent with the breeze. Then, when the winds gathered in force, they snapped the umbrellas' thick posts like toothpicks. Telephone wires began flapping like thin strings on swaying poles. The rain started to pound so hard that it sounded like drumbeats on the pavement, rooftops, and car hoods.

It is one thing to know something is about to happen, but it is another to feel at peace with it. And though Jenniemae might have predicted that this storm was headed for the area, it did not mean that she felt at all tranquil. As the weather went from bad to worse through the afternoon, Jenniemae kept repeating, "Oh Lord, the train's a-comin', the train's a-comin'. And Lord help us now. Lord help us now." When the wind gusts picked up ferocity, the windowpanes rattled and the outside black shutters, which were commonly hooked into the side of the house, came unhinged and banged against the wood siding. "Lord have mercy now."

Things—big things, small things, red ones, blue and black and yellow things—flew by the windows of our suburban house, almost as if half of Washington was being blown into Maryland or Virginia. Small dogs or even large cats could easily have been picked up and carried off with this wind if they weren't huddled safely inside.

Only Jenniemae and James were home that day, and as the storm continued to blow and tree branches could be heard snapping outside, Jenniemae began to sing in order to drown out the noise and calm her nerves.

> *You'll be hearin' the trumpets sound*
> *To wake all that be underground*
> *Look into God's right hand*
> *When those stars fall to land.*

And while Jenniemae was trying to occupy her mind by singing and straightening up almost anything she could find to straighten up and praying to the Lord not to put an end to the world quite yet, James was in his study, working. He seemed to have been hard at work all morning. Jenniemae knew he was working on something, but she never would have asked or even cared exactly what that was. Their relationship wasn't about what or how each did at work—it was about what or how each did in life.

By late afternoon the rain began. Thunder could be heard rumbling in the distance and then white streaks of lightning began to light up the sky. Jenniemae stopped what she was doing and stood very still in the middle of the room. Moments later there was a loud crack and then a roaring crash could be heard in the front yard. Jenniemae went to the window and saw that one of the tall, old maple trees had toppled and was lying on the ground—a tree that had probably stood in that spot for more than a hundred years.

Jenniemae muttered, "Lord Jesus." The rain seemed to be coming down now in waves and splashes. The lights flickered. James then appeared in the living room to join Jenniemae.

"Damn big storm, isn't it?" he said, and then noticed the maple tree. "Look at that!"

Jenniemae nodded and said, "Lord knows it's a shame to lose that tree, just a shame. No more shade on that side of the house."

In the distance they could hear ambulances and fire trucks screaming. The streets were undoubtedly flooded and tree limbs had to be strewn everywhere across the city. This was not a good day to travel.

"Katariina is on her way here now," James said, and Jenniemae just replied with, "Um-hum. That's one more gust."

"What does that mean?" he asked.

"Nothin'. Just talkin' about the storm here," she said.

"No you're not, Jenniemae. You know you're not. What are you saying?"

"Well, Mister James, far as I can tell, she *is* the storm."

"Don't be ridiculous."

"Maybe. And maybe not. That's how I see it."

"That is absurd. She's a nice girl who is out there caught in this storm."

"Lord," she said, and shook her head. And then the lights flickered on again for a few seconds and then off again, until they went out completely.

The two of them stood silently in the middle of the room. It wasn't dark now, but it would be within a few hours.

"We better get the candles and matches out," he suggested.

"Sure enough."

As they were opening drawers looking for candles, James

asked Jenniemae, "You think this has something to do with Katariina, don't you?"

"Well . . ."

"I know you do and it's crazy thinking," he told her.

"Maybe so, maybe not. But Mister James, what matters to me more is how you go and worry on her so much and not on your family enough. That's not right."

"I don't think that's at all true," he defended himself.

"Oh, but it is true, Mister James. Lord knows it is."

He didn't reply. James knew that there was no use in arguing with Jenniemae, whether or not she had a point. She would think what she would think and he couldn't change her mind about it. Both of them were stubborn with their notions and both of them knew that about the other.

The afternoon light began to fade and the house grew darker. Jenniemae lit a few of the candles. "Best to have some light," she said.

"Okay, that I will admit is a fact."

"Lord you know I'm right."

"Lord I don't think you're right."

"Don't say His name if you don't mean it."

"All right, then, you're just wrong," he said, and she shook her head.

They sat in the living room—she on a red velvet-covered chair and he on the long beige couch—for a long time without saying a word. Finally James broke the silence.

"You've heard what's going on?" he asked.

"Some things. A piece of some things," she said, not certain what he was going to talk about—but fairly sure.

"So you knew already that Missus Ruth has been thinking about leaving me?"

"Well, now . . . I had a sense it might be happenin' . . . and, well, then that there is one bad thing, isn't it?"

"Marriage isn't easy, is it?" he said.

"Guess not for some folks. But you could make it easier now."

"Are you advising me?" He smiled.

"No, Mister James. You have got to do that all by yourself."

"I suppose I will, then. I know you don't like Katariina, but you have to remember that you don't really know what another person is doing and why he is doing it unless you are that person."

"That's the truth. That is the truth and I appreciate what you are saying, but you sure go out of your way to make your own life a misery."

He laughed. "Maybe. Maybe it's just the way I want it."

"Maybe so, Mister James. Maybe so."

"Why didn't you ever get married?" he asked.

She laughed, and he repeated his question.

"Lord, now." She thought about it for a moment. "I guess it never seemed like the right thing for me to do. Never the right man and never the right time. I didn't ever and don't ever want to be married just to be married, Mister James."

"Smart."

"Maybe yes and maybe no. Maybe smart and lonely," she admitted.

"Are you ever lonely, Jenniemae?" he asked her.

"Oh Lord . . . I don't know. I got my Lila and I got my sister and nieces and nephew and I got John-John now and then, but *lonely* is a word that comes in different ways at different times of the night. You know what I mean, Mister James?"

"Yes, absolutely."

The two of them stopped talking and watched the flickering light of the candles. They sat in silence, and when the electricity came back on, both rose from their seats. The lights were on and it was a different world.

# CHAPTER TWENTY-SEVEN

*"Man's gonna find*

*what he's not lookin' for*

*because he's not lookin' for it."*

It was 1960, and as the new decade commenced, it seemed as if the country was entering adolescence; everything was about change. The mood—from fashion to politics to rock and roll— demanded "out with the old and in with the new." The nation as a whole seemed impatient and rebellious. The civil rights movement was no longer going to be satisfied with slowly grinding forward in first gear. People wanted reform and they wanted it now. The concept of "black power" would emerge, and black power meant civil rights and black power also meant voter rights. The black vote in the United States, which never before had seriously influenced the outcome of any election, was about to make an enormous difference. In 1960 a young, attractive, and charismatic senator from Massachusetts, John F. Kennedy, ran against a less attractive, staid vice president, Richard Milhous Nixon. The race would be extremely close—120,000 votes separated the two men—and many believe that had it not been for the Kennedy endorsements by black leaders Martin Luther King Jr. and Ralph

Abernathy at the last minute, which clearly influenced black voters, it is very possible that Kennedy would not have won. By 1960 the space race that had more or less begun in 1957 was in full throttle; the United States and the Soviet Union raced to become the first nation to set foot on the moon. In 1960 the Food and Drug Administration approved the birth-control pill, which helped usher in the sexual revolution. The musical wave of the sixties saw the introduction in the United States of the "Fab Four"—the Beatles—whose songs soon occupied top positions on the *Billboard* Hot 100 list. President Kennedy began his administration by announcing the creation of the Peace Corps, which was intended to involve young Americans in the problems of foreign nations, and young and old both had a glimmer of hope.

Although the decade began with an air of excitement and promise, it soon revealed its serious side. Within six months of Kennedy's election, the country was on a collision course with Cuba. The United States' ill-conceived secret storming of the Cuban coast—the Bay of Pigs invasion—led the nation toward the brink of disaster when the Soviets responded by installing nuclear-tipped missiles in Cuba aimed at the United States. Tension mounted and many Americans believed that the country was heading toward Armageddon. At the same time, another conflict thousands of miles away was brewing, as the United States became more involved in South Vietnam. Although South Vietnam got little media attention in the early 1960s, the fighting there would soon become a weighty war—and a war that would ultimately put the nation on its heels. The 1960s was not going to be a simple or a quiet decade.

Shortly after Kennedy's January inauguration, life began to change in our house also. Ruth left James on a Tuesday night. Katariina left him on Wednesday afternoon. In fact, the two women had designed their leaving in this way. They'd spent weeks discussing when each would leave, who would leave first, what would be said or left unsaid, and how they would communicate with each other after both were out of the house. Though Jenniemae had predicted that something was going to happen, she certainly hadn't been let in on their plan. And while this plan was a secret kept between Ruth and Katariina, no one—including James—would have said that it was particularly surprising. He was well aware that each departure was a possibility, particularly given the difficult and volatile relationships he had with both women. His relationship with Ruth had been colder than usual, and he had been fighting constantly with Katariina. So when both women left, he was only mildly surprised. Indeed, the same could have been said for me—I was not at all astonished, given the friction in the house. However, I was a bit unprepared for the way my father reacted; rather than feeling distraught, he seemed to feel relieved. Ruth and Katariina had left. The house was quiet for once. He didn't have to deal with an angry wife or a difficult lover, both of whom had been consuming his energy day and night. For once he didn't have to deal with either woman's demands or desires, which was something he hadn't experienced for a long time, if ever. He didn't have to worry about heated arguments that led nowhere. He didn't have to take care of another person's needs or feel guilty for what he did do as well as what he didn't do. The house wasn't filled with an air of discontent, noise and commotion—all of that walked out the door with these women. He mentioned to Jenniemae that it was one of the first times he could just do what he pleased when he pleased and not have to explain it to anyone. "Not a care in the world. I can eat macaroons for lunch and drink whiskey for dinner. Tell me how that is bad."

"We'll see how long that suits you," she warned.

"I don't know, but today is good enough for me. It has been said before that pleasure is no more than just the intermission of pain, and perhaps that is all too true. More reason to seize on the limited time that any intermission affords us."

"Maybe so. I hope your intermission time lasts a long while, then," she told him.

Over the next weeks James made the most of his newfound free time. During the day he threw himself into his work. In the evenings he filled his time by playing chess or reading or visiting friends. He began to craft a new life, a life without women, and rather than fall apart, he seemed happy and delighted with himself. Friends were shocked to see how happy he was, but few thought it would last long. Jenniemae called this time "the danger time" and said that if James weren't the kind of man who seemed to want many of the things that he shouldn't have and have many of the things that he shouldn't want, things might turn out differently. "When he doesn't have what he doesn't need he is still lookin' for it, and when he's finally up and got it—he is in misery. There is not never goin' to be any peace in that."

She was right. The tranquil air that had settled in the house—that intermission, the period of happiness and seeming freedom from stress—did not last long. After a month, or maybe a little over a month, James's persona of tranquillity evaporated; in fact, it disappeared so quickly that it almost seemed as if he'd never gone through this happy, serene period. It was strange. When he was happy it seemed as if he might remain calm and happy forever—or at least for a long time—and then when that time ended, it seemed as if it had never happened in the first place. Why James's life changed all of a sudden was a mystery. There didn't seem to be any one thing in particular that demarcated the change that took him from a quiet, tranquil person back to one whose life was filled with noise and tension. Maybe he read something profound that changed his mind, maybe a friend telephoned and suggested something that altered his point of view, maybe he suddenly felt forlorn and lonely, maybe it was something he ate or something he drank or too much that he drank. Or maybe it wasn't anything in particular. Whatever it was, it happened just like that—almost overnight, really. One night James seemed completely happy and relaxed and the next morning he was in knots.

It was true that James wasn't a man who would be content with contentment for very long. Jenniemae had that right. Ultimately he would fall back into the pattern of wanting to have what he should not have. No matter that being alone made him less tense and more productive, he seemed to have a need to bring the craziness back into his life. The peacefulness finally made him more nervous than the craziness ever had. Peacefulness was just too damn peaceful. The quiet was too quiet. He understood the craziness. He was comfortable with it. When the house was tranquil, James believed he was missing something—something he absolutely needed or emphatically had to have. Jenniemae said she had never seen a man who was so bent on making a mess of his life.

"You don't need to make a mess of things now, Mister James. Just settle with the quiet you got. Just settle for a while longer and see how it goes before you jump into another hornet's nest."

"I'm not looking to make a mess of things."

"Oh, yes you are. I can see it and I can hear it buzzin' in your head."

"I'm not as foolish as you think."

"That's the truth, 'cause you are *more* foolish than I think."

"I'm fine."

"No you're not. I can see you can't even stand livin' with your own skin."

"What does that mean?"

"Jus' what I said. You can tell by lookin' at a man's skin if he is comfortable or not."

"Is that right?"

"It is. A man that doesn't fit into his own skin is lookin' for trouble."

Jenniemae worried about him but knew there was little she could do. He was restless. He looked for solutions to his restlessness everywhere—in his work, in finding other women, in getting back together with Ruth, in rekindling the Katariina relationship, in drinking whiskey, in driving cars too fast.

Jenniemae would hear him on the telephone with Ruth, trying to get her to return home. In truth, James had mixed emotions about whether he wanted Ruth to return. It was clear that he still loved her. He also resented her, respected her, and admired her, but she was never going to be enough. This was a man who needed more than she—or any one woman—could ever give. To complicate things, Ruth was involved with another man. So he turned his attention to Katariina and began to telephone her more often than he did Ruth. He begged her to come back for just a week or even a weekend, even though he knew that relationship would bring him nothing but turmoil and grief. They argued on the telephone for hours and sometimes through the night. The arguing became the relationship. Katariina, who had returned to her family's home in Gary, Indiana, was conflicted. For whatever reasons, Katariina did love James. Even though he was almost three times older than she and that they had little in common and that he was a married man with children her own age—she still did love him. She wanted to return, she didn't want to return. He wanted her back, he didn't want her back.

Jenniemae hoped and prayed that Katariina would find someone or something new and just disappear from James's life. But unfortunately for Jenniemae's peace of mind, things didn't turn out that way. One morning she arrived at work only to see Katariina's baby-blue Jeep—the one that James had bought her months ago—parked in the driveway.

"Oh Lord," Jenniemae groaned as she entered the house. "Man has a mind to hurt hisself. Man has a mind for hurt. Lord, Lord, Lord."

Katariina stayed for almost three months before she and James began to argue again. At one point she wanted him to divorce Ruth and marry her, but he refused to do that. At another point he promised her that one day they would move from the area and buy a house together, but she refused to believe him. They argued about money and clothes and cars and other women and other men and about sex. They went away on long weekends, driving the new deep-green Aston Martin into the Virginia countryside, and would then return united, only to start arguing again days later. For almost the entire time that Katariina stayed at the house, Jenniemae barely uttered a word to James. She went about her work trying to avoid him whenever possible. If they crossed paths, she pretended to be busy dusting or straightening up—she wouldn't look him in the eye. He understood the silence, though he chose not to confront it. And of course Jenniemae refused to utter a word to "the foreign girl" and would never once look her in the eye, either. There was no point in speaking with someone you couldn't stand to even look at. This uncomfortable situation could not have gone on forever. Jenniemae considered how long she could last before she would reach her breaking point and speak up. She wasn't about to let this situation go on indefinitely. She watched as their relationship began to dissolve, and though she hated to listen to their arguments, she hated it even more when they got along well. And whenever they seemed to be kind or loving with each other, Jenniemae occupied her thoughts by silently gambling on how long they would last before the next fight broke out—how many days would go by before they'd begin to bicker and argue, and how many days before the entire mess imploded. However, when things did truly begin to get out of hand with

Katariina and James's arguments, Jenniemae became extremely uncomfortable. It was one thing when they yelled and screamed at each other and doors could be heard slamming upstairs, quite another when the fighting turned physical. And it did. One morning James came downstairs with a cut on his cheek and a black eye. He told Jenniemae that he had fallen down the stairs the night before, and though Jenniemae didn't want to become involved in what had happened, she also wasn't going to let him lie to her face.

"Now, Mister James, I am no fool. I know what I see and I see what I know."

He didn't say a word.

"And I'll tell you something, Mister James. And you listen to me here. A man that looks for trouble is always goin' to find it. You understand me? This is no way."

"I know," he said quietly. "I understand."

A few mornings later Jenniemae arrived at work and the blue Jeep was gone. She breathed a deep sigh of relief. When she walked into the house, James, standing in the kitchen, told her, "Katariina left."

"Thank the Lord for that."

"It's better this way."

"Yes indeed it is, Mister James, and I hope you can keep that in your mind. The only time you go and act like a fool is when you get mixed up with these ladies here, there, and every which where."

"Maybe."

"It's the truth. It *is* the truth."

And not a word more was said about Katariina, though Jenniemae expected that she just might return one day. With Katariina out of the house, Jenniemae worried that James might try to quickly replace her with someone else and that one morning she might arrive at the house and see some strange woman there. And one thing Jenniemae did not like was surprises. She felt that surprises usually came on the heels of bad luck. A surprise was something you didn't expect and usually, in Jenniemae's mind, the thing you didn't expect was more often than not bad luck. One afternoon she warned me, "Your daddy's gonna find what he's not lookin' for because he's not lookin' to find what he needs."

"How do you know?" I asked her.

"I know by watchin' him, honey, and you do, too." Jenniemae was right about that. I did know even if I didn't want to admit it.

"Is he ever going to change?" I asked her.

"Not likely. Now, when was the last time you ever seen a leopard without his spots?"

"Never," I answered. "So what do we do about it?"

"Remind him when he's bein' a fool. Lord knows that's what we need to do. Remind him all the time," she said, chuckling.

As the weeks went by, both nothing and something occurred. Katariina did not return and Ruth didn't, either. Yet the atmosphere, which one might have expected to have been calm, was anything but that. Jenniemae said we were waiting again for a lightning strike. "You know it's gonna come, just don't know when or where it's gonna hit. Just keep an eye out, honey. Somethin' is gonna happen. It is."

I knew she was right about this. I don't know what I expected or what Jenniemae expected, but I think I knew that things would not remain as they were for long. Something would happen. A new woman would appear or perhaps a new car or three new cars, or maybe he would buy a new house—something.

But when that something did occur, it threw both Jenniemae and me off.

One afternoon, while Jenniemae was preparing dinner, James casually asked her, "Would you consider staying here for a few days?"

"What?"

"I just thought that perhaps you could stay here for a few days," he repeated.

"What do you mean, stay?"

"Stay."

"Stay where?"

"Here."

"Why would I go and do that?"

"Well . . . I thought it might be nice."

"Nice? How is it nice? Nice for who, Mister James?"

"I just thought it might be a good idea. I'm not saying you have to do it."

"I know that. I know I don't have to," she said, raising an eyebrow.

"Just think about it. It wouldn't be forever. Just for a few days—a week maybe—to make things easier. And I would pay you more," he added awkwardly.

"Why?"

"Why what? Why pay you more?"

"No. Why would you want to have me stay here?"

"Why not?"

"Because I can't do that," she told him.

"Why not?"

"Because I can't. I have my life and you have got your own . . . and what am I going to do here?"

"I don't know. Just be here."

"That's right. You don't know. You don't need me to be here more than I am. You are jus' fine even if you don't think you are. A few days isn't goin' to change anything at all. It makes no sense."

"How about you just consider it. Just think about it before you decide," he asked.

Jenniemae knew him far better than most people did, and she knew that asking her to come stay in the house wasn't easy. But she really didn't want to stay overnight for one day, two days, or three, and she had a feeling that he thought he might be able to manipulate her into staying longer once she came for a few days. And she most certainly did not want to live in our house. She also didn't feel he needed her there, either. Jenniemae further understood that sometimes Mister James got a thing in his mind—like thinking that it would be a good idea for her to stay overnight in the house—and even if it was a wrong and crazy notion, he became stuck on it and couldn't give it up. It was another one of those times when he would go and do a thing that he didn't need to do, a thing that wasn't good for him to be doing in the first place.

"It makes no sense at all," Jenniemae said. "You don't need to have me here, and if I did come you would hate it. You don't want me here. I know you don't. I know you jus' got it in your head that you don't like the way things are quiet in the house, and so you want to up and change things around, but this is no way. Nothin' is gonna change by my stayin' here. Nothin'. You understand what I'm sayin' here, Mister James?" she asked him directly.

"Maybe."

"No *maybe* about it. How about you take a trip for a while and visit some of your friends. You go on up to that New York City and see some of your people up there and then this feeling might go away," she suggested.

"I don't want to take a trip. All I am asking is if you would think about staying here for a few days."

"Oh Lord . . . All right, then, I'll think on it," she agreed, "but don't keep askin' me every five minutes."

By then I was fifteen years old, and Jeffrey was in New York in his freshman year at Columbia University. I had just gotten my learner's permit. I was secretly smoking a half a pack of cigarettes a day, sneaking my father's whiskey on the weekends, stealing the car keys and taking the Thunderbird or the Aston Martin out when he wasn't home. Having Jenniemae come to stay in the house—no matter how much I loved her—was, to say the least, not what I wanted to have happen. I could still smoke behind the garage, and most likely could get away with it. I might be able to sneak liquor, but taking one of the cars would be virtually impossible and, at the time, I considered that to be one of the most important events in my life. Driving the winding roads through Rock Creek Park late at night, heading down to the Lincoln Memorial, driving Constitution Avenue around the reflecting pool and then crossing over the Memorial Bridge to Virginia and speeding along the George Washington Memorial Parkway at sixty-five, seventy-five, eighty-five, or ninety-five miles an hour was what I commonly did when my father was out. So when he announced that Jenniemae was going to stay with us for a while, I was not at all pleased.

"What do you mean, Jenniemae is coming to stay with us?" I complained.

"I thought you would be delighted with the arrangement. For a couple of days there will be someone here when I'm out. And not just anyone—it will be Jenniemae."

"Are you serious? What's a couple of days going to do?" I distrusted that a couple of days meant a couple of days.

"I thought you would like it. You won't be home alone every night."

"We don't—well, I don't need to have her here. I'm fine alone. I like being alone. I hate having other people here. A couple of days is ridiculous," I argued. I never did fully understand why he wanted to have Jenniemae come and stay—it never did make a lot of sense. He always cherished his privacy, and no matter that he adored Jenniemae, it seemed out of character. It occurred to me that, ironically, he might have been doing this for my benefit— at least in part for my benefit. I think he felt guilty about going out almost every evening and my being left at home alone, and though he didn't want to give up his going out, he also didn't want to feel guilty about it, either. But I was fifteen and, as I reminded him, I didn't need a babysitter. However, his viewpoint and appreciation of my being fifteen probably didn't match my viewpoint or appreciation of being fifteen. He saw me as sweet, innocent, guiltless, sinless, faultless, vulnerable, and alone. I, on the other hand, didn't see things that way. I was not sweet, was most definitely not guiltless nor sinless nor faultless, was somewhat innocent, extremely gullible, and very vulnerable—but I was not as alone as he thought. However, there was another factor that may have been at play when he asked Jenniemae to stay at the house, and that was that it had something to do with his just wanting more women there.

In any event, Jenniemae did come to stay with us, and that one day became two days and then the two days became three. And then an entire week had gone by and then it was coming on two weeks. For me, two weeks of not doing what I wanted to do seemed like an eternity. I missed stealing the cars late at night. It wasn't easy to smoke or drink with Jenniemae around since I was always worried about getting caught, and getting caught by Jenniemae would have meant disappointing her, which would have been unthinkable. And even though I knew that Jenniemae wasn't going to stay too much longer—she had Lila and her life to return to—I hated not knowing when this would come to an end. Jenniemae stayed because she was asked to by my father, but I think her biggest motivation for staying was that she felt sorry for me being home alone. No matter what Jenniemae went through in her life—and she went through a lot of very tough times—she always had her family. There was always someone to turn to, always people in her house, always someone to cook for or eat dinner with or talk with, there were always sisters, nieces, nephews, brothers to turn to—always someone—and the idea of being alone was foreign to her and she didn't like it for me, either. Knowing this, and also knowing that Jenniemae really didn't want to stay in our house any longer, I was the one who finally brought the issue up.

"You know I am fine here alone at night," I told her one afternoon. "You really don't have to stay any longer. Really. I'm fifteen. I don't need anyone here. I'm fine." And she was unquestionably relieved because the next morning she told my father she was not staying any more nights.

"I got to get back to my own. I got my life and you got yours, Mister James. Now, maybe if you want someone here, you should go and ask Missus Ruth to come on back. She might like that and you might like it, too."

"I understand," he told her.

"I mean that about askin' Missus Ruth."

"I doubt she would want to return."

"You never know if you don't ask," Jenniemae suggested.

Four weeks later, my mother returned.

# CHAPTER TWENTY-EIGHT

*"It takes a heap of licks to strike a nail in the dark."*

Almost everyone was affected in one way or another by the changes taking place during the sixties, whether you were a farmer in Iowa, a mechanic in Indiana, or a broker on Wall Street. For his part, James decided it was time to change his personal style: He updated his formal wardrobe and instead of three-piece suits he dressed in sports coats and casual shirts and discarded his bow tie. He sold his Rolls-Royce and bought the new DB6 Aston Martin. This Aston Martin was steel blue. He bought a new two-speaker stereo radio and decided that rock and roll would be heard throughout the house in the afternoons. Besides the Beatles' "She Loves You" and "I Want to Hold Your Hand," there was Johnny Cash's great song "Ring of Fire," Roy Orbison's "Mean Woman Blues," Lesley Gore's "It's My Party," and the Ronettes' "Be My Baby." Those were the tunes the local deejay played over and over again that James liked to crank the volume up for. But he had his dislikes, too: He didn't like the Surfaris' "Wipe Out," Jan and Dean's "Surf City,"

Jay and the Americans' "Only in America," or Gene Pitney's "Twenty-Four Hours from Tulsa."

As for James and Ruth's lives together, I am not certain whether they had grown older and were simply too exhausted to fight or whether they learned to accept each other for who they were, but they fought less than ever before and seemed to enjoy each other's company more.

That is not to say that they were entirely settled with their lives, though. Ruth stayed in touch with her boyfriend and James always kept his eye out for the next lover. Ruth, a successful practicing psychologist in D.C., now traveled extensively to conferences in San Francisco, Santa Fe, London, and New York. She also was extremely involved in a program at the NIMH (National Institute of Mental Health) with the renowned psychologists Fritz Redl and Bruno Bettelheim, and taught part time at American University in D.C. and at the University of Maryland in Baltimore. In 1965 she co-authored with Nicholas Long and William Morse a successful book, *Conflict in the Classroom*. James both admired and hated Ruth's successes. As much as he may have been frustrated by her dependence on him years ago, he most assuredly found her successes far more difficult to accept. He disliked her feisty independence and self-confidence, particularly as he struggled with his own work. He complained about her travel and often allowed as how the dogs had more empathy to offer him than she—a successful psychotherapist— and that the dogs required of him no more than a bowl of food served on the floor twice a day. However, they stayed together. Perhaps, during those years, it could be said that they needed each other in many ways more than they actually loved each other. She didn't really want to be with her new lover more than she was (not to mention that he was married), and James seemed satisfied with Ruth being available sometimes but not too often so that he could go out with his new girlfriends.

However, ever since the publication of *The World of Mathematics* in 1956, James had been plagued with self-doubt. Could he repeat his success with another blockbuster? Could he just repeat with a good book? Could he produce anything? Was he finished as an author? Who would listen to him or read what he wrote? Who cared about the history or philosophy of mathematics? Who wanted to read about mathematicians or proofs or mathematics in general? There was a war brewing, a civil rights movement growing, a sexual revolution blossoming—who gave a damn about mathematics? The more he doubted himself, the more he doubted himself. In 1961 he published *Science and Sensibility*, a collection of his essays on science, philosophy, mathematics, and civilization that expressed his belief that the essence of any culture is in the interaction of science and the humanities. The book was well received by critics but never sold the way *The World of Mathematics* did.

In the wake of this publishing disappointment he threw much of his energy and passion into the political firestorm surrounding the nuclear armament race and the potential for nuclear war. The public reaction—or lack thereof—both frustrated and infuriated him, as it always had, but now even more so. As had been true since 1945, when the first atomic bomb was detonated, politicians and scientists argued over the possible dangers and ethics of atomic or nuclear warfare. The arguments intensified and usually concerned (and still do) whether or not the United States, or any nation, should build up a stockpile of weapons that amounted to what was euphemistically called an "overkill arsenal." In the 1960s, the public remained largely uninformed and dangerously ignorant about the weapons stockpile that the government was considering increasing. The absurdity of the notion of building such a stockpile unsettled James.

In addition, during the summer of 1961 international tensions had mounted between the Soviet Union and the United States, and in particular between Soviet premier Nikita Khrushchev and President Kennedy. Tensions rose to such a degree that Secretary of Defense Robert McNamara, under Kennedy's leadership, had asked Congress for $100 million in order to build public fallout shelters. James was infuriated by the idea of the administration's shelter program and wrote a brilliant and sarcastic letter to *The Washington Post*:

## Noah's Dilemma

Occupied the other morning with my fateful two-by-two selections I almost missed the morning newspaper which reported that the Secretary of Defense, Mr. McNamara, had asked for shelters to save 10,000,000 lives. This is, it need scarcely be said, a heart-warming action and I offer Mr. McNamara my congratulations, congratulations which

I hope will warm his heart. Still I do not envy him the task that lies ahead, so difficult to execute, so vexing to administer, so demanding in its choices. Will there be a shelter for my aunt? What about the Mayor of Chillicothe? May I bring my dogs—assuming I am among the chosen? And if my dogs have a place will it deprive the three boys who live two flights up in a brownstone on the southwest corner of 74th Street and Amsterdam Avenue in New York City? What a dreadful dilemma.

I am not unacquainted with it. For some time now, as I indicated, I have been making a list. Let me assure Mr. McNamara that the problems of a modern Noah make the earlier chap's problems seem as simple as selecting the proper boxes for noughts and crosses. My plan was straight enough. Make a list, assemble the creatures to be saved, rent (I suppose charter is the proper word) a ship, load it, sail south. Below the equator would probably serve as a safe haven. I have been reading meteorology, to learn about prevailing winds, and anthropology, to find out where the natives are friendly. As an American, it seems to me, I would have no trouble getting a warm reception. There were many logistical details to be worked out, such as refrigeration (fortunately, I realized I would not have to take penguins because they are south already), shipboard games, food, and so on, but I was confident I could take care of them, and I thought it likely if I were sincere some Higher Power (in the Administration or further up) would sooner or later give me good advice. Several A.E.C. publications might be useful, though they have a way of going out of date, a Bible perhaps, a sextant and some flares. The main thing, however, was positive thinking. I was not going to ask what anyone could do for me, rather, what I could do for anyone.

Yet in the last analysis the necessity arose of making tormenting choices. Two by two is all very well, but which twos? Start with the lower forms and work up. I had decided early on to take only organic matter and leave behind books, musical scores, antiques and so-called cultural objects. If necessary, I resolved, they can be made over again, besides, where would I ever find room for a Lincoln rocker? A closer question was what to do about plants. I could not take a pair of giant sequoias— they've lived long enough anyway—but what about roses and chrysanthemums and lilies of the valley and thistles and lettuce and all the other plants, including bacteria? That, you can imagine, was a poser. But I solved it. Take seeds, I said to myself; they keep better than animals (some spores, I am told, can slumber for thousands of years, and are as good as new with a little sunshine and water) and you can plant them where you are going.

If they grow, they grow. If they don't grow they don't deserve to grow. Natural selection, and a fine thing too. As for the bacteria, I concluded that the animals would bring a full assortment. That was off my mind.

I was pleased with myself. Now for the animals. This, I confess, turns out to be quite a challenge. Beetles, for example. There are more than 60,000 species of them alone. Did I really have to have two of each? Well, a thing isn't worth doing if it isn't worth doing well, and this was a case where the thing was worth doing well. O.K., 120,000 beetles. I'd manage somehow. Viruses? Some are bad, some good, but who am I to judge? Take the viruses. Snakes? Yes, snakes. Vicunas? Where would I find two vicunas? I fancied the curator of the Washington Zoo might not understand, but I hope he would give me one vicuna and I would get the other from Tulsa. Secretary birds? Must have a pair. Zygotes? I don't know what they are but I resolved to have two. Smith's frog: two. Elephants? Two, I'm afraid, preferably small. Asiatic horned toads? No. Let Asia take care of itself. Pheasants? A brace. Salmon? By all means, but only the fresh water varieties, because the fish in the sea can survive without my attentions. Turtles? Certainly. Hummingbirds: beyond doubt. Rabbits? Positively not; myxomitosis would be better. Deer?

An enchanting couple. Anteaters? Yes, but must remember to keep them away from the ants. Barnacles? They would come without urging. Eagles? American. Buffalos? The last chance before we really extinguish them. Puffins? Wouldn't be without them. Bees? A full set with queen.

And so I made my list of things that swim and fly and wriggle and walk.

Now I come to us, the crown of my difficulties—and Mr. McNamara's. Two of each state of the Union (including Hawaii)? Or just two model citizens in good health, one male, one female? A pair of blonds and a pair of brunettes perhaps. Two dark-skinned persons? Two children? Two Texans? Two from each country of the Free World? What about the unfree world and the uncommitted world (medium latitudes)? Do I really have to take two Albanians? Two Chinese or four Chinese? Two Germans or four Germans? And what of the Berliners? After all, they are a special case, for whatever else happens, if a war should break out, the people of that stronghold of freedom and liberty will vanish altogether. How hard it is, I reflected, to fill the cup before life's liquor in its cup be dry.

There it is. Poor Mr. McNamara. His choice is in a sense harder than mine. Two of each: that at least is a discipline. Just two, no more, no tears, do the best you can. But 10,000,000. Good Heavens! The number is so large, the time so short, that nothing less than a lottery, a randomized computer, or some form of bingo—to be held in churches—will suffice to surmount the problem. And imagine the disappointment, when the number is large, of the 170,000,000 or 180,000,000 who are left out. Nevertheless I am sure the Establishment will be able to make it clear to the remainees why they had to remain; and there will be no grumbling if they are told honestly what is at stake and how much better off they are this way than the other way, whatever the other way may be.*

A month later James wrote another angry letter to *The Washington Post* and *The New York Times* attacking the ludicrousness of stockpiling weapons.


## A Modest Proposal

I address myself to the Eminences and the Sereneties. I make them a Modest Proposal. Let our children go.

---

*James R. Newman, "Noah's Dilemma," *The Rule of Folly* (New York: Simon & Schuster, 1962), pp. 55–58.

A nuclear war, which day by day seems more likely, may very well end human life. But suppose, more cheerfully, that only the people of the Northern Hemisphere are exterminated; that in the Southern Hemisphere it will still be possible, somehow, for some persons to survive. Why should we not transport our young children to these regions as a refuge? The merits and advantages of the Proposal are obvious and many, as well as of the highest importance.

For first, as I cannot conceive of any sane person capable of human feeling would challenge, the war to come, if war comes, is not the children's concern. Our quarrels, our bitterness, our hatreds, our fears do not possess them. Our heroes and our devils are not theirs. They have barely begun their lives, they are not ready to end them for Causes. They are too innocent and foolish to realize that death is preferable to life under alien creeds. I recall a story which Carl Sandburg told of a little girl, perhaps his granddaughter, who, after hearing his description of a battle of the Civil War, observed, "Suppose they gave a war and no one came." There is no reason to suppose that children, unless forced, would come to our war.

Secondly, the conduct of the war would be so much less Burdensome if the children were removed. It would be necessary to yield to niceties, to observe amenities, to nurse the sick, to shield the weak, to spare the infirm. With the children gone, without the distractions and temptations of their cries and complaints, we could give ourselves over completely to the serious business at hand. There would be many fewer mouths to feed, less need for water and air and bandages and whole blood. Children are notoriously subject to epidemic diseases; thus a prolific source of infection would be eliminated.

The savings in money alone would be immense, and would not only pay to transport the children and maintain them until they could fend for themselves, but would leave a handsome margin for use in vigorous prosecution of the war. I have made a rough calculation for U.S. children which bears on the point. Say we take many of the children from the ages of two to twelve—the younger are too frail, the older are more stable and could be useful to us at home—then we shall have about 25,000,000 to transport and keep. For this purpose, allow $1,000 a head. The total is $25,000,000,000, a sum well under half our annual military appropriation. Surely this is not too much to spend, considering the advantages to be gained.

Thirdly, we rid ourselves once and for all of the Incubus of a shelter program. What a relief no longer to have to pretend! What a comfort simply to face the facts! No sensible person, even among scientists, believes in the efficacy of shelters. Down one goes to the well-stocked, cozy hole. Then what? There is the gentle patter of fallout on the roof; one is shielded from the blast; the light of a thousand suns (or is it now a million suns?) does not penetrate. The Lares and Penates are there. The family is snug. Father is pedaling the air-pump. Mother is preparing a tuna-fish casserole. The radio is on. Splendid. But when does one come up and what is there to come up to? Anarchy? Cannibalism? The living dead? Bloated corpses? Troublesome questions. And even more trouble-some is the effect of fire and heat, a subject which none of the experts and no one in the Establish-ment has seen fit to discuss. I lay this omission, of course, to delicate feelings. It would, I believe, un-dermine morale to be reminded of the fire storms over Tokyo, Hamburg, Dresden, where a mere few thousands of tons of high explosives produced atmospheric convulsions.

Now with weapons, each of which may yield the equivalent of ten, or fifty, or a hundred million tons of high explosives, the fire storm produced by a single bomb will, I am reliably informed by an arti-cle in *Scientific American*, vaporize the structures and burn off the vegetation of an area of at least 15,000 square miles. Even in a deep shelter the occupants will be quickly barbecued. What a dreadful thing to contemplate. It is enough to make cowards of us all. The necrophiles, the bitter ones, the incandescent patriots, those among the aged and ailing who take comfort in the thought that their demise will coincide with that of mankind: these endorse the view that shelters will give shelter. But secretly they laugh at our innocence. We must not encourage them. If we are to die for the Cause, let us not cheapen and betray the sacrifice: Away with the shelters, and all will become clear.

Fourthly, there is the grave moral issue of suicide. The law forbids it to the individual. On a national scale, however, it is apparently acceptable. Do we not, after all, make the law? Thus we may write its exceptions. Still the question nags us, can we require the suicide of those who have no voice in the making of the laws, viz., children? It is a fine point, and none would venture to say how our leaders would feel compelled to decide it. My Proposal disencumbers them of this obligation.

Fifthly, there must be many who, like myself, have a Weakness for children. In format and freshness they are much preferable to the larger editions, their parents. Children are unwrinkled, unwarped. They are healthy. They smell nice. They are not cynical. They suppose life to be an end in itself. Properly nourished, watered and cared for, they grow up. When grown they can breed. The dead do not breed. Quite recently the eminent geneticist Herman Muller described a scheme for setting up large scale sperm banks. Sperm could be stored indefinitely; it could be classified according to the characteristics of the males who produced it. Human evolution would thus, in a sense, come under man's own control. Yet the scheme presupposes the continuance of women. It is my impression that sperm by itself will yield no fruit. Here again the Proposal is vindicated; for there will be female as well as male children; instead of storing germ plasm we will be storing the young themselves and thus assure the future.

For the moment I have said enough. I am anxious that Wise men consider my Proposal. Is it Feasible? (Less feasible, say, than a journey to the planets?) Is it visionary? (More visionary than the preservation of Freedom by nuclear war?) Is it too Costly? Is there time to execute it—in part at least if not in whole? Could it be made a matter of International Cooperation? Is a country without children worth living in? Perhaps not. In that case some better course must be found. Let the Wise men define it.*

---

*James R. Newman, "A Modest Proposal," *The Rule of Folly* (New York: Simon & Schuster, 1962), p. 64.

James spent much of his life immersed in the struggle to bring reason and ethics into the forefront of any discussion about weapons and warfare. The fervor he had for this issue was something he never would give up. And he was certainly an important and prominent figure among the group of men and women who joined in this effort—Linus Pauling, Jonas Salk, Benjamin Spock, I. F. Stone, Eric Fromm, to mention but a few.

Yet as involved and passionate as he was when writing about the arms race, he had a far more difficult time succeeding with his books in the way he had before.

In early 1963 he'd published *The Harper Encyclopedia of Science*, which was intended to be a standard in the field, to be re-edited and re-issued every couple of years in order to offer current information. It sold only moderately well. In the introduction for that book he wrote:

> *Felix qui potuit rerum cognoscere causas*: Happy is he who has been able to learn the causes of things. Virgil's epigram was made in a happier time, a more innocent time, at any rate, when men supposed that while many causes were not known, yet in due course they could with diligence and ingenuity be found out. Of this we are no longer certain. The physical universe is a queer place— queerer, as it has been said, than we can even suppose. The more we know of it, the more we realize how little we know of it. The solid ground of Nature is a delusion; any of the comfortable, scientific

truths we were raised on have been disproved and the rest will assuredly share this fate. Physics and astronomy, once so secure, are now in a marvelous chaos; biology and chemistry have in half a century been almost unrecognizably transformed; there has come into being in a few decades a veritable giant of science, biochemistry, which promises to decode the intricate ciphers of living processes; and even mathematics has been drastically renovated and will never again be regarded as a temple of eternal verities. A scientific theory, as we now believe, has a major purpose: to be demolished. It can never be proved correct; it is useful to the extent that it suggests experiments which will help disprove it.*

After *The Harper Encyclopedia of Science* was published, James worked on a biography of Michael Faraday. Faraday, an Englishman, lived during the early and mid-nineteenth century. He was a chemist and physicist whose discoveries in the fields of electricity and magnetism led to the viable use of electricity. Though Faraday was considered to be mathematically naive, his complex work with electromagnetic theory was mathematically astute. On a personal level Faraday was, for the most part, unlike James. He was a devout Christian, was married once,

---

*James R. Newman, *The Harper Encyclopedia of Science* (New York: Harper & Row, 1963), p. vii.

was not known to have had other lovers, and had no children. Like James, however, Faraday was politically active. Faraday fought against both the industrial pollution of the Thames and the air pollution of London. James's fascination with Faraday did not have to do with the man as much as with his work, which formed the basis of magnetic field theory.

James struggled with this biography. Some days he spent hours in his office successfully working and others he couldn't work at all. It may have been that he had chosen the wrong person to write about. It wasn't that Faraday's work wasn't interesting or important, but Faraday's life was not as exciting as that of many other scientists or mathematicians he might have chosen. He mentioned to me once that the work on Faraday was often tedious. He began to avoid working on the project, and the further it slipped away, the harder it was to return to. Once again he became depressed. Without a steady lover he had more time to obsess about what he wasn't doing with his life. He obsessed about not being able to work, he obsessed about never again being able to work, he obsessed about thinking about working. And he became more and more obsessed with how much time he had left to live. He realized—or at least he believed—that time was not on his side. It was highly unlikely, he felt, that he would live another twenty years—or another ten— or maybe even another two. Although this wasn't exactly a new feeling, it felt more pressing now. His sense of paranoia, like a sleeping dragon, was acute. He questioned everything: the world around him, the nature of Nature, the nature of mankind, the ability of anyone to change the course of events in the world, his own ability to change the course of events, his chances of living through the year or the month or the week or the day. While life on any given day was good, it couldn't be taken for granted since it would most likely turn sour at any moment. And if life was already bad, then that should be expected, though it would likely get worse soon.

During this time both my brother and I graduated high school and left for college. The house was quieter than it had ever been before. Jenniemae still came to work every day though there was less work to do. Still, there never would have been any question about her remaining with the family and being paid the same salary no matter that the work load was less. However, during this period, when she noticed that James had once again become despondent—again retreating into what she called his "danger place"—she made a conscious decision not to coddle him. Those days of coddling were past, and given all the time they had spent together, she felt she should and could speak her mind. With each passing day James turned more inward and became more silent, working less and walking less. He retired into his bedroom early but rarely slept. The light in his room remained on throughout the night as he read books, one after the other—mysteries, novels, biographies, history books. He played chess by himself. He read every page of the newspaper. He lay awake staring at the ceiling. He checked his pulse often. Many mornings he would rise from his bed having slept not one minute. Jenniemae didn't like the way things were going one bit.

"Mister James, you're fallin' again," she confronted him. "You don't look good. You're not sleepin', are you?"

He didn't respond, so she continued. "You can't jus' let this hammer fall on you."

"Hammer?"

"Hammer. Rock. Don't matter what it is, Mister James. Don't matter what you call it."

He said nothing.

"You know where it's gonna get you. You know it. Nowhere is where. Nowhere."

"Maybe," he said.

"Don't 'maybe' me. You're jus' gonna go into that dark place where you can't see out and we can't see in."

"And?"

"It takes a heap of licks to strike a nail in the dark, Mister James, and that's exactly what you're doin' now, strikin' in the dark. You understand?"

He stared off as if listening to some other voices.

"Are you listenin' to me?"

He turned and said, "No."

"Lord. You are impossible. You have to stop this. You have to stop listenin' to those voices in your head that are leadin' you off to some no-good place. Everybody has those voices . . . you jus' got to shut them down sometimes. Shut them down and get back to work. The difference between your voices and mine is that you listen to yours and I don't pay attention to mine. I'm not about to pay attention to craziness. You understand? You think you're the only one with voices?"

"I don't know."

"Well, you're not. I got voices. We all got them."

"Is that right?"

"You know it's right, Mister James."

Jenniemae left him alone for the rest of that day. But before she left work she tried again to force him to snap out of this spiraling depression. And the next morning she lectured him. Ruth tried to connect with him and then she invited a few of his friends to come over to try to pull him out of his dark space. When it was suggested that he might be ill, Ruth called the doctor, who paid a house call and, realizing that James hadn't slept in over a week, prescribed sleeping pills. But Ruth feared that he might just use them to overdose.

I was in college and though I had a sense of what was transpiring at home, I did not know the details. My mother telephoned to ask that I return home right away. She felt frightened by my father's behavior and his waning health, and realizing that I was one of the few people who might be able to pull him out of his current depression, she wanted me there. I doubt that my mother might ever have considered that Jenniemae might have the ability to sway him one way or another. I don't believe my mother felt completely helpless on this occasion, but I do think she felt somewhat paralyzed when it came to influencing or altering the moods or habits of her husband. Rather than attempt to change his behavior on her own, she frequently chose to either deny what was unfolding or to ask others to help out. It was understandable to some degree—over the years she had become emotionally ground down by their difficult relationship and had come to feel incapable of being able to give him what he needed or wanted (and probably some of the same could have been said for his feelings about her). My mother's asking for me to come home and "rescue" my father seemed like the obvious solution—at least in her mind—though it clearly was one of those instances in which she probably overstepped a boundary between what was my life and what was her life. Nevertheless, she needed my help, telephoned and asked me to return, and I left school right away, catching the first possible train to D.C. From everything I had been told on the telephone, I thought my father must by dying. But when I arrived home I wasn't so sure that was the case.

As pleased as he was to see me, he was also very surprised and immediately questioned why I had left school and what I was doing at home. "Why are you here?" he asked me.

"Because Mother asked me to come home."

"Why?"

"She's worried about you."

"Why?"

"Because."

"Because? Is that all?" He smiled.

"I guess so."

"Then there's nothing to worry about. If it is only 'because,' then you should return to school. I'm fine because or not because. You understand?" My father had a way of making sense out of nonsense.

"I understand, but I'm going to hang out here for a few days."

"Why?"

"Because." I smiled and he laughed.

"Fine."

The first few days I was home, my father and I took long

walks together through Rock Creek Park. In the evenings we played chess or watched television, but our conversations were always limited. He didn't care to discuss how he felt or what he was thinking and I doubt that I would have liked to have heard it, anyway. And though I didn't believe he was dying, it was obvious that he didn't look well and was clearly depressed. His skin was pale, his usually rosy cheeks were gaunt, and deep, dark rings were drawn beneath his eyes. He wasn't quite as meticulous as was common for him, his hair was thinning and grayer than before, and even his clothing was sometimes untidy. Toward the end of the week he insisted that I return to school. Whatever he was feeling or going through—and as much as he enjoyed my company—he most certainly didn't want me staying at home. I also wanted to return to school and asked Jenniemae for advice: "What should I do?"

"You can't stay down here, honey. You got to go back to school. Your bein' here is gonna make him angry after a while more. I know it and you know it. And there's another thing to remember."

"What's that?" I asked her.

"Honey, the day a leaf falls in the water is not the day it spoils. Nothin' is never over and done with until it's really over and done with. You understand?" she asked.

"I suppose so."

"You go on back to school, child. I know what I know," she told me. "He will get back up on his own and in his own good time. You go on back. He ain't gonna die now."

"You sure?"

"I'm sure."

She was right, because he didn't die. After about a month in that dark space he seemed to regain himself and come back to life again. He began working, walking, talking, and laughing again. Who knew what caused the turnaround—I doubt even he knew. But he did return. He began to work again on his biography of Michael Faraday. And Jenniemae advised that "it is best not to try and understand something that is not meant for understanding," which I believe might have been one of the most important of the many lessons she offered.

# CHAPTER TWENTY-NINE

*"Better is the good end of a thing than a bad beginning."*

In 1965, James was invited to give a commencement address at Johns Hopkins University. It was not the first time he had given an address or been given an honorary doctorate degree or spoken before a large audience; however, it was the first time that he invited his family to join him. Johns Hopkins was only a forty-minute drive from Washington, D.C. Because the event didn't require extra airline tickets or hotel rooms, we were invited to attend.

Jenniemae was stunned when James invited her to come to the Johns Hopkins commencement ceremony. She had never been farther than five miles outside the city of Washington since she moved from Alabama. How long would it take to get there? What would she wear? And was he sure the Johns Hopkins people knew who he wanted to bring along? Those were only a few of the questions she had as soon as he posed the question.

"Are you foolin' with me, Mister James?"

"No. I want you to come."

"I can't do that."

"Sure you can."

"It makes no sense. No sense at all. I won't get what you're talkin' about."

"Yes, you would get it, and that doesn't matter, anyway. No one listens to these speeches."

"What?"

"No one listens to speeches at these ceremonies. They just sit there and stare into space wondering when the speech is going to be over and what they're going to have for lunch."

"That's not the truth."

"Sure it is."

"Mister James, I can't come and you know why."

"Why?"

"Why? Because."

"I want you to come."

"Am I there for you to make one of your points now? Because I'm not no Rosa Parks."

"I know that. It has nothing to do with making a point. You're invited because I want you there. And since when do you give a damn about what other people think?"

"Since always, Mister James. Since always."

"Don't think about it so much. Just come along."

Jenniemae thought about that for a minute. "Lord. I don't like this."

"You will like it."

"No I won't."

"Please come."

"Oh, Lord have mercy."

"Good. Terrific," he quickly replied.

Jenniemae was pensive for a few moments. Then nervously she asked, "What do I wear?"

"Wear?"

"Yes."

"Anything," he said, not knowing how to respond.

"Can I wear my hat?" she asked.

"Hat?"

"Yes. My hat. Can I wear that?"

"No. Don't wear a hat."

"Why is that? Why can't I wear my hat?"

"People sitting in the rows behind you don't like to look at hats." She laughed. "I never had anybody sit behind me."

"Well, you will now. Lots of people sitting behind you."

"Lord have mercy."

"Don't worry."

"I will worry."

"There's nothing to worry about."

"Where is Baltimore?"

"North of here."

"North? How far are we going north?"

"Not far. Don't worry. It's not far and it's not exactly in Baltimore."

"Then where is it exactly?"

The speech was scheduled to be delivered May 10. Jenniemae fretted about every aspect of the event. She thought up excuses for not going—she was feeling sick, the weather would be bad for her arthritis, her cousin was sick. She was nervous about what she would wear, how long the drive was, what it would be like sitting in one of those tiny chairs that were not made for women who weighed 350 pounds, how she'd feel sitting in front of hundreds of white people—literally in front of them—and what it would be like to listen to Mister James talking. The only time she had been in an audience listening to someone was when she sat before her preacher, and even then she was usually standing while singing with the choir.

A few days before the event Jenniemae arrived looking more worried than was common for her. Before Ruth left for work she told her, "Missus Ruth, I don't think I will be able to go to Mister James's talk."

"Really? Why not?"

"Jus' can't. Y'all go and have a good time. I can't do it. Better is the good end of a thing than the bad beginning of it."

"Jenniemae, we want you to come. And this is not a bad beginning."

"No. It is a bad beginning. I jus' can't go. I'll feel out of sorts."

"You'll be fine."

"How am I goin' to look?"

"You mean what would you wear?"

"That's right."

"Oh Jenniemae, don't be silly."

"I'm not bein' silly at all."

"All right, then, I get it. Here is how we're going to handle this and, please, no arguing. I am going to give you some money.

It is for you to buy a dress for yourself, and we're never going to talk about it again. Never a word."

"Oh Lord, I can't do that."

"Sure you can."

"Missus Ruth."

"We won't talk about it. We'll just do it."

On May 10 a shiny black limousine arrived at our house. The driver parked in the driveway, got out, and stood at the limo's back door, waiting for us. James, looking dapper, wearing a fashionable dark-blue pin-striped suit, light-blue cuff-link shirt, and black-and-blue striped tie, got into the front seat—he enjoyed traveling in the front seat of taxis or limousines and speaking with the driver just as he always enjoyed speaking with the garbagemen, the deliverymen, the postal delivery men, the plumber, the roofer, the street paver. As much of an intellectual and an elitist as he was, he also enjoyed listening to what the man on the street had to say. He could spend hours unraveling mathematical mysteries and he could also spend time talking with the garbageman about his children.

Jenniemae wore a cotton pink dress that had small white flowers all over. The dress had long sleeves with white ruffled cuffs and a matching white ruffled hem that hit just below her knees. She wore white patent-leather shoes and white gloves and she carried a wide-brimmed pink hat rimmed with white flowers, even though she knew she couldn't wear it. Her graying hair was pulled back into a tidy bun. She looked very pretty.

"You look lovely," Ruth told her as we traveled along on the Washington-Baltimore Turnpike.

"Well, thank you, Missus Ruth. You do, too," Jenniemae said, commenting on Ruth's new white linen suit, which she indeed did look stunning in. "You always do."

"Thank you, Jenniemae."

"Are we in Maryland?" Jenniemae asked, staring out the window at the unfamiliar landscape.

"Yes. Still in Maryland."

"Do we leave Maryland?"

"No, we're going to stay in this state."

"Well, that's a good thing, then. Not good to change too many things all in one day."

"You know what they say, Jenniemae?" Ruth asked.

"What's that?" Jenniemae always loved a new saying.

"Everything flows and nothing stays. You can't step twice into the same river."

"Ain't that the truth. Ain't that the truth."


Johns Hopkins had never suggested what James should speak about during the address. And none of us had asked. The university may have assumed that he would speak about the importance of science and mathematics in developing new technologies or about the role of science and mathematics in civilization. Given his political involvement, they may have expected him to speak about the war in Vietnam or to touch on the civil rights movement and the sense of change in the country. He didn't choose any of those topics, however. He wanted these future scientists and mathematicians to question the relationship between science and society and to always recognize the obligation that scientists have to remain diligent in adding morality and ethics into the mix of scientific methodology. As he expressed it:

> It is a commonplace that science is not wisdom; that it may save us from the pox but not from our own folly. But like many other commonplaces this one is not very helpful. Indeed, it is a source of much mischief because it promotes the cause of fashionable philosophies which assert that, since science cannot provide answers for all human problems, it is not a safe guide in dealing with any of them. We all agree that science has changed civilization and will continue to change it if there is a civilization left. But we do not agree—and on this point scientists no less than other thoughtful men fall out among themselves—as to how knowledge can be used for good ends and what are the responsibilities of its discoverers to see that it is not used for bad ends. Science cannot resolve these issues but scientists have no right to evade them.*

---

*James R. Newman, *What Is Science?* (New York: Simon & Schuster, 1955), p. vii.

# CHAPTER THIRTY

*"When you dream,*

*that dream is the truth,*

*and when you wake,*

*that truth is nothin' but a dream."*

The day after the Johns Hopkins address, Jenniemae thanked James for inviting her to hear his speech in Baltimore.

"Did you enjoy it?" he asked.

"Yes I did. I liked that you talked about men being responsible with what they do, Mister James. You know I like that."

"I thought you might."

"And by way of a thank-you, I have something I would like to give to you," she told him.

"You don't have to do that."

"I know I don't but I want to."

"That's very nice."

"I think you'll like it. And you can put it to use."

"Really?" he said, curious.

"It's a number and a horse," she told him.

"What number?"

"It's the Saturday racing horse."

"Saturday? You mean the Preakness? The horse race on Saturday?"

"Yes. That's what it is."

"How did you know the horses run on Saturday at the Preakness?"

"I know what I know. And that limo driver mentioned a thing or two about it."

"Is that right? And you think you know who's going to win?"

"Yes I do. I know."

"Okay. Which horse is it?"

"It's number six, Mister James. Number six is my best number, and that is what it's goin' to be. Tom Rolfe is the horse. He is goin' to win that race. He's got number six."

"Really?"

"Yes it is. Tom Rolfe. Number six. So you have to be there and bet on him."

"You want to go?"

"No. I want you to go. You take Missus Ruth and you bet on number six. Tom Rolfe."

And on Saturday, May 17, James and Ruth went to Pimlico Race Tracks to watch the running of the Preakness. James bet on number 6—Jenniemae's favorite lucky number. The horse was Tom Rolfe, ridden by jockey Ron Turcotte, and Tom Rolfe won the race. James won $950. The next day he gave Jenniemae half of his winnings.

"Do you want to gamble on the Belmont?" he asked her. "It's the next big race."

"I don't gamble. I got the dreams. Gamblin' is the child of

greed, Mister James, but dreams—they are the children of the soul."

"I only know what I see every day and it looks like gambling to me."

"A dream is not a gamble. I know what I know. And I know that when you lie down at night and you have a dream, then that dream is the truth, and when you wake in the morning, that truth is nothin' but a dream."

# EPILOGUE

On May 28, 1966, James R. Newman died of a heart attack. He was fifty-eight years old. Ruth was at home with him that night. She reported that the last words he spoke were to the paramedics when they gave him a shot of morphine and put him on a stretcher: "Morphine is the answer when dying seems to be the question."

I was about to graduate from Sarah Lawrence College in Bronxville, New York. My father had been asked to deliver the commencement speech. Obviously that never happened. A memorial service was held in Washington three days later. Thousands attended, including friends, family, prominent physicists, mathematicians, publishers, editors, writers, teachers, Supreme Court justices, federal judges, senators and House representatives, film directors, actors and actresses, former lovers—and, of course, Jenniemae.

Alan Barth, a good friend and a man who served on the editorial board of *The Washington Post* for thirty years, spoke at the memorial service. I believe a few of his words sum up much of the man my father was:

> Jim was full of extravagances. I always marveled that, in spite of the exceptional subtleness and suppleness of his mind, he was incapable of neutrality or even indifference. What he disliked, he abhorred; what he disapproved, he condemned beyond all possibility of redemption. There were no compromises in him. Perhaps it is not entirely fanciful and sentimental of me to think of him as a little like Cyrano de Bergerac: insufferably sensitive to slight, absurdly romantic for all his sophistication, brilliant yet sentimental, a little grandiose in manner, imperious to the strong yet gentle to the weak and forever at war with hypocrisy and cant and compromise, an implacable foe of pretense and pomposity, a fighter for the sake of fighting and because he was incapable of coming to terms. For all his ferocity, Jim had a gift of friendship. He did not give himself to many. But he gave, when he did so, with great generosity, great loyalty, and with unstinting affection. Those he loved could scarcely do wrong in his eyes. Greatly gifted, he was great troubled. He was abrasive as well as brilliant. And in some ways, of course, he troubled all those whose lives he touched ... he was above all else himself—restless, eccentric, unique— in the true and primitive sense a mensch, a man.

Another good friend, I. F. Stone, the infamous investigative journalist who published *I. F. Stone's Weekly*, remarked:

Jim was arrogant, unkind, overwhelmingly egocentric, and often impossible. He was also irresistibly charming, enormously gifted, and endlessly fascinating. Conversation with him tended to become a monologue, but no monologist ever had more to say that was perceptive, rewarding, and amusing. His idea of a really appropriate and enjoyable memorial service would be for all his friends to get together over champagne and whiskey and exchange affectionate but witty and slightly malicious reminiscences of Jim when he was at his most unendurable self.

Ernest Nagel, a leading philosopher of science, and the co-author with my father of *Godel's Proof,* remarked:

Jim was a teacher by native endowment, though his teaching was done mainly through the printed word. He could make complicated ideas intelligible without ponderous technical jargon, but also without emasculating their content. He once wrote a description of Einstein that I cannot think more fitting of Jim himself: "He felt for humanity and deeply sensed himself a part of it, sharing its hopes and fears. He hated war—the atavist instincts that produce it, the

degradation it causes, the suffering it inflicts. . . . He
was a skeptical man, contemptuous of dogma, properly disrespectful of authority. . . . He regarded science as a discoverer and a liberator. It would open the
world and teach men how to live and to be happy."

My father left a professional legacy of an impressive body of
work, but he also left a personal legacy that has taken me many
years to understand. And I still work at it. The essence of the
man did not lie in his work or in his tangled relationships with a
multitude of lovers; rather, it lay in his deep sense of loyalty to
the people he loved and in the quick and wicked sense of humor
he used to ease the tensions of a complex life.

My mother outlived my father by three decades. She died
from heart failure and emphysema. The cigarettes that were her
best friends ultimately turned out to be her worst enemies. She
was a remarkable woman who influenced and touched the lives
of many people personally and professionally; a brilliant, complex woman with a crazy sense of life and living who was not
always the best of mothers but was always one of the most cap-
tivating, honest, and modest of women I will ever know.

Jenniemae continued to work at the house until she became ill
in January of 1969. She died two months later. I was at her bedside on the day of her death, and as I sat beside her that afternoon,
she told me, "Honey, when that door opens and I go one way and
you go the other, don't you worry, because I am always listenin'
and watchin' and I can hear what you need to tell me. But it's up
to you to listen on back. You understand? Listen on back."

# ACKNOWLEDGMENTS

There are a number of people I would very much like to thank and acknowledge for seeing me through the eight years it took to write this book. First and foremost, I cannot imagine having completed this without the encouragement and suggestions made by Michael Korda, who reassured and emboldened me from the very beginning of the project. I also cannot adequately thank Sterling Lord, who believed in this project even when it was a mess of an idea. He fortified me when I needed it most and never gave up. Without a doubt, I owe an incalculable indebtedness to Nancy Doherty—without her extraordinary editorial skill and advice I would probably still be struggling with this or that chapter. And then there is John Glusman, who edited this book by making me feel as uncomfortable as hell, and who saw to it that this discomfort would make the book better. I dreaded his telephone calls, which forced me to work harder, obsess a bit less, and get it done right. And I am grateful to Anne Berry and Domenica Alioto for walking me through this process. I also want to thank Anne Bernays for her constant support and Justin Kaplan for his thoughtful, wonderful advice, which was absolutely "right on." Without a doubt, I owe more than words could ever express to the woman who rescued, grounded, encouraged, loved, and fortified me: Bea Liebenberg.

Unquestionably, I could not have completed this manuscript without the patience, the tact and also the lack of tact, the advice, and the reassurance of my children—Joey, Blue, Samantha, and Nikos. They heard many of these stories so many times that they could have easily written their own book (which may happen in due course!). And then, not at all last or least, I owe deep-seated gratitude to my husband, Mark LeRose, who did not simply encourage me to keep going—he demanded it with love and respect.

BROOKE NEWMAN is the mother of four children and lives and writes in Aspen, Colorado. She is the author of *The Little Tern*, a fable for adults that has sold more than a million copies worldwide.